Do You Know God's Will For Your Life

?

by
Jim Barbarossa

Step by Step Ministries
215 Sauk Trail
Valparaiso, IN 46385
219-762-7589

ISBN 0-9676380-0-3

Published by Action Pubications, Inc
P.O. Box 21690, Keizer, OR 97307-1690
(503) 463-1992
E-mail: robeson@webcombo.net

Table of Contents

Table of Contents

ACKNOWLEDGEMENTS

*Thanks to our friends for helping us
proofread and correct this manuscript.*

Norm & Kathleen Rasmussen
Pastor Dan Nicksich
Sharon Marrs
X-Press Printing

SPECIAL THANKS

*To all of you that helped pray me into God's Kingdom.
As we go forth, you share in the fruits of our labors.*

SPECIAL! SPECIAL! THANKS!

*To the man that showed me how to be a witness for
Jesus. . .a man that is a true minister of reconciliation.*

Brother Ray Moore

SPECIAL! SPECIAL! SPECIAL THANKS!

*To my wife and best friend Carla, for praying for my
salvation for nineteen years, giving me four wonderful
children, and being my partner in life and in service to
God.*

BIGGEST THANKS OF ALL!

Thank You, Jesus!

Do You Know God's Will For Your Life?

Finding God's will for our lives is not as complicated as we sometimes make it to be. Actually God's will is very clear.

GOD'S WILL = GOD'S WORD!
GOD'S WILL = THE BIBLE

As you read this book, every time you see the words

GOD'S WILL:

Read what it says. Then apply what it says to your life. If it is not clear to you, ask God to show you through the Holy Spirit how to apply what you read into your life. To help you apply God's Will (the scriptures) into your life, ask yourself these questions.

1. Is there an example in this for me to follow?
2. Is there a sin for me to avoid?
3. Is there a command for me to obey?
4. Is there a promise for me to claim?
5. What does this passage teach me about God? About Jesus? About the Holy Spirit?
6. Is there a difficulty here for me to explore?
7. Is there something specific in this passage that I should pray about?

Take time after every scripture to ask yourself these questions. It will be time consuming now, but it will help you to find God's Will for your life. Don't just read this book. Meditate on it. Talk to God and let Him talk to you.

CHAPTER 1
The Jim
Barbarossa Story
"Be His Witness"

At one point in my life I became very sick. I missed twenty out of twenty two months work on the job I had held for nineteen years. I was having symptoms ranging from severe headaches to dizziness and light headedness. I lost the vision in my right eye for a time. I had stomach cramps and constipation. I had lumps underneath the skin that would just pop up anywhere and nobody knew what they were. They would break open and drain. I laid on our couch for months just waiting to die. Finally, my doctor sent me to the Mayo Clinic and they ran some tests. They diagnosed it as a rare blood disorder called Mastocytosis. Basically it was an over production of histamines within the blood stream.

GOD'S WILL:
> *The thief cometh not, but for to steal, and to kill, and to destroy: I am come that they might have life, and that they might have it more abundantly.*
> *John 10:10*

The devil was trying to kill me, but Jesus had another plan, which was Life; and that more abundantly.

We had been blessed with many "things." We had a nice house, cars, a lot of toys: snowmobiles, campers, and other possessions. But there was something missing deep down inside. I chased after it and could not find it. I looked in bars, on the softball field, and in racquetball courts. I worked 16-hour days and made more money. I started my own business, then another business. I chased, looked and searched but nothing could fill the emptiness that I had deep within me. I thought, *"There has to be more."* I missed something somewhere, but I just didn't know what it was. I had placed all of my possessions at the center of my life; they were my god. I had turned my back on God and was headed for hell. It scares me now to think how close I was. Anything could have happened at any time and I would have been gone.

One night, about three o'clock in the morning, we got a call from a good friend. His father had suffered a heart attack. Something happened within me and I prayed. The only thing I can figure out is that it had to be the leading of the Holy Spirit, because I had never done anything like that before. If I had, it would have been for selfish reasons. It would be for myself, not for somebody else. I prayed and said, *"Lord, this is a good man. This is the kind of man You can use to lead someone like me to You. God, if you'll save him, I'll be in church on Sunday."*

So on Friday or Saturday of that week I said to my wife, *"Don't make any plans for Sunday night. We have something to do."* She was puzzled. I don't think she could figure out what was going on, or what was so important about Sunday night. But when I went to church with her I think it answered her questions. It was probably a shock to her. At the end of the service I didn't want to go home. I really felt comfortable. I felt at peace. There was a calmness and I was really enjoying it.

The following Sunday night I went back. I was sitting in the last pew at the back of the church, the closest one to the door, the one where you can quickly get away. There was an altar call given and I wanted to get up, but I couldn't move. It was as if I was glued down. In my heart I wanted to get up, but something would not release me. So I prayed and said:

"God, if You want me, You'll have to send someone to get me." It seemed but a couple seconds that a lady came to me and said, "Jim, do you want me to pray with you?" I said, *"Yes, I do."*

GOD'S WILL:

Ask, and it shall be given you; seek, and ye shall find; knock, and it shall be opened unto you:

Matthew 7:7

I went to the altar and I confessed my sins and asked Jesus Christ into my heart. I threw my hands up and said, *"God, I want everything You have and I'll give You everything I've got!"* My life has not been the same since. God is good! It was the best thing that ever happened to me.

GOD'S WILL:

That if thou shalt confess with thy mouth the Lord Jesus, and shall believe in thine heart that God hath raised him from the dead, thou shalt be saved. For with the heart man believeth unto righteousness; and with the mouth confession is made unto salvation.

Romans 10: 9-10

It was during this time that I had to leave the job that I had held for twenty years because of my medical problem.

About 6 months after coming to know the Lord, I found a lump on my chest. I went to the doctor and he said to come back in two weeks. *"If it is not gone, we're going to do a biopsy and see what it is."* He gave me some medication. But I don't think he thought it would really do anything.

So I took the medication for two weeks. I was due to go back to the doctor on Monday — it was Sunday night, an hour before service. I was taking a shower. I looked in the mirror and the lump was as big as it was the day I went to the doctor. While standing in front of the mirror I remembered a scripture. *"By His stripes we are healed."* I looked at the lump, said: *"I don't have to have this. Jesus paid the price."*

I got dressed and went to church. I went up for prayer, and several people came up and laid hands on me. As they prayed, the power of God came upon me and I was slain in the Spirit. Lying on the floor, my hand was on my chest and I could feel the heat between my hand and the lump. It was like a warmth.

One hour later, I went into the men's room and opened my shirt and that lump was the size of a freckle and the next day it was gone. Praise God! We have a healing miracle-working God. My doctor was amazed.

GOD'S WILL:
Who his own self bare our sins in his own body on the tree, that we, being dead to sins, should live unto righteousness: by whose stripes ye were healed.

I Peter 2:24

Four months later, while kneeling at a communion service, I heard these words go through my mind:

"My son, this night as you confess your sins before me, I wash them away with the blood that was shed for you on the cross and with that same blood I am now cleansing your diseased blood. You will go back to the doctor and the disease will be gone."

Six weeks later I went back to the doctor. Tests were ordered and the results came back that my blood was normal. **I am healed!** Praise God!

GOD'S WILL:
But he was wounded for our transgressions, he was bruised for our iniquities: the chastisement of our peace was upon him; and with his stripes we are healed.
Isaiah 53:5

One day while in the bank I found a wallet lying on the counter. I took it to the teller and she thanked me profusely. She said, *"Nobody would have brought this back and turned it in."* I gave it to her and went to my car. As I was getting in the car, the Holy Spirit said to take my testimony and give her one. I took two; one for the lady who lost the wallet and one for the teller. I didn't think anything about it after that.

A week later my wife was in the bank. She didn't know what I had done, but the teller said, *"I want to thank you so much for your husband's testimony. I want to tell you something. That empty feeling that he had, that void; I have that in me, too. Can I come to church with you?"*

We ended up at her house and prayed with her. She made a recommitment to serve the Lord and she is now in church.

GOD'S WILL:
And they overcame him by the blood of the Lamb, and by the word of their testimony; and they loved not their lives unto the death.
Revelation 12:11

Last year my wife and I built a mini-storage warehouse. I met a gentleman who also owns one. While driving by his warehouse, I was led to go in. Even though he doesn't have an office on site, he was there so I left a couple of testimonies. I left them with him and told him a little bit about my life and what God had been doing. This was in February. In May I ran into him in a store. I didn't recognize him because he looked different. He came up to me and said, *"Guess what? I go to church now."*

I said, *"You do? Tell me about it."*

He said, *"Do you remember that little red Bible you gave me? I sat it on my desk in February. Three weeks ago I was sitting at my desk and had a feeling that I should pick up that little red Bible. I was looking through it and I felt something go through my hands. I didn't know what it was."*

I said, *"Brother, you were touched by the Holy Ghost."*

He shared that with his wife. She had been born again one month earlier. She said, *"I felt that, too, but the only time I ever felt it was in church. I want to feel it at home."*

God is good. It was the leading of the Holy Spirit. A step of obedience on my part is what it took and my brother was blessed.

GOD'S WILL:

But ye shall receive power, after that the Holy Ghost is come upon you: and ye shall be witnesses unto me both in Jerusalem, and in all Judæa, and in Samaria, and unto the uttermost part of the earth.

Acts 1:8

The greatest thing that has ever happened in my life is receiving Jesus Christ as my Lord and Savior. There is nothing that compares. That's the ultimate.

The second greatest thing that I have ever experienced in my life is being allowed the privilege to be used as an instrument of Jesus Christ; to help lead somebody else out of darkness into His marvelous light.

We were traveling and went into a waffle house restaurant. Everything went wrong. What we ordered, they didn't have. My wife ordered a piece of pie with ice cream and they said, *"Well, there is a convenience store down the street and you can get the ice cream and bring it back."* My son wanted a hamburger with french fries and they didn't have any fries. Whatever we wanted — they didn't have it.

A man walked in and sat down behind us. He started talking about the weather. Then he talked about a man he used to hunt with, who was in his nineties. He told us the man had passed away and he had never gotten over it. He told us when he was in Vietnam, he was in a foxhole and he knew if he had died there he would have gone to heaven because Jesus Christ was in that fox hole with him.

But the sad part about it was, here he was back in America, in a restaurant, and he left Jesus Christ in that foxhole. You could tell he was a lonely and hurting man.

My wife looked at him and said, *"You know what? Jesus is still here. You can have Him right now."* But he started talking about some other stuff.

Then it was about time for us to leave and as we were walking out of the restaurant, my hand hit the door handle and the Holy Spirit stopped me, turned me around and said, *"Go talk to that man."*

I went back to him and laid my hand on his shoulder and said, *"Brother, I don't want to leave here today until you have Jesus Christ back in your heart where He's supposed to be."*

He said, *"Well, keep me in your prayers."*

I said, *"How about we do one better than that; we'll pray for you right here and now."* Then, we received an unexpected blessing. We had our three sons with us as we were talking with this man, our sons were saying, *"Dad, can we go get the Bible? Can we go get a tape? Can we help?"* They saw the value of what we were doing. They knew how important it was for this man to be right with the Lord and they wanted to help; they wanted to partake. That was really great!

We ended up praying with the man and he received Jesus Christ back into his heart right there in the middle of that restaurant.

GOD'S WILL:
And I, if I be lifted up from the earth, will draw all men unto me.
John 12:32

Later, during our vacation, I felt led of the Lord to pick up a hitchhiker. His leg could not bend and he had a hard time getting in my truck. He said he was going to a bar a few miles away. I did not want to take him to a bar but I felt God was in it so off we went. He told me he had been hurt 18 years earlier and that's why his leg would not bend. As we went down the road, God spoke to me to tell him that God had not given up on his leg. So I told him. We went down the road a little farther and I was impressed to tell him again. About that time I felt led to tell him how God healed me of an incurrable blood disease.

As I finished my testimony, he said *"This is where I get out."*

As he got out I said, *"God has not given up on you, and I'm going to pray for you."* He got out and headed toward the bar. Suddenly he stopped, turned around and came back to my truck.

He said, *"When you pray, pray for my back. The nerves were damaged and that is why my leg does not bend."*

As he walked back to the bar, I jumped out of the truck and said, *"I want to pray for you."*

- 8 -

He said, *"Now, right here in front of this bar?"* I said, *"Yes!"*

He asked, *"But what will you do?"* I said, *"I will lay my hands on you and ask God the Father in His son, Jesus' Name, to set you free, to heal you."*

GOD'S WILL:

And these signs shall follow them that believe; In my name shall they cast out devils; they shall speak with new tongues; They shall take up serpents; and if they drink any deadly thing, it shall not hurt them; they shall lay hands on the sick, and they shall recover.

Mark 16: 17-18

He said *"Do it."*

So I prayed. I felt God's power all around. After praying, I took him by the hand and said, *"I believe God is going to do something for you."* I went back to my truck where my father-in-law was waiting and watching.

He said, *"What did you do to that man?"*

"What do you mean?" I answered.

"The man just went past the bar and is going back in the direction we brought him from." The Power of God kept him out of that bar!

At that time I looked in my rear mirror and saw the man going down the road. Guess what he was doing? He was shaking and bending that leg that had been damaged for eighteen years. The power of God healed him and set him FREE! God sent me five hundred miles to pick this fellow up and pray for him. That's the love and power of God.

Obedience to the Holy Spirit is probably the most important part of my testimony. The message that the Lord has given me is to challenge people to respond to Him in obedience by doing exactly what He says when He says it.

GOD'S WILL:
If ye be willing and obedient, ye shall eat the good of the land:

Isaiah 1:19

GOD'S WILL:
And Samuel said, Hath the Lord as great delight in burnt offerings and sacrifices, as in obeying the voice of the Lord? Behold, to obey is better than sacrifice, and to hearken than the fat of rams.

I Samuel 15:22

Jim's story, about his salvation and healing is available on the audiocassette tape,
"The Healing Testimony."
See Item #1 on order form in back of book.

CHAPTER 2
Is There Something Missing In Your Life?

Is there something missing in your life?

WHAT will FILL the VOID, the gap, the empty place within you?

(1) **MONEY can't fill it!**

(2) **GAMBLING can't fill it!**

(3) **BOOZE can't fill it!**

(4) **POPULARITY, BEING THE LIFE OF THE PARTY can't fill it!**

⑤ **DOPE can't fill it!**

⑥ **CIGARETTES can't fill it!**

⑦ **PLEASURE, HOLIDAYS, VACATIONS can't fill it!**

⑧ **SPORTS can't fill it!**

⑨ SEX can't fill it!

⑩ FRIENDS can't fill it!

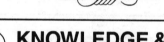

⑪ KNOWLEDGE & DIPLOMAS can't fill it!

⑫ YOUR JOB, YOUR PROFESSION, BEING A WORKAHOLIC can't fill it!

⑬ RELIGION can't fill it!

⑭ FAMILY TRADITIONS can't fill it!

GOD'S WILL:
For God so loved the world, that he gave his only begotten Son, that whosoever believeth in him should not perish, but have everlasting life. **John 3:16**

⑮ only JESUS CHRIST...

can fill it!

God has put a desire for Himself in the heart of every person and only God can fill that desire.

Everyone has an empty space inside of them which needs to be filled. You can try any one of these examples *(maybe you already have!)* Their satisfaction is only for a short time and you are always left with the same need!

GOD'S WILL:

He has made everything beautiful in its time. He has also <u>set eternity</u> in the hearts of men; yet they cannot fathom what God has done from beginning to end.

Ecclesiastes 3:11 NIV

God Is Eternity.

God has placed eternity in the heart of man. God has put a desire for eternity (for Himself) in the heart of every person & only God can fill that desire.

There is, however a Person who is able to FILL THAT EMPTY PLACE WITHIN YOU.

GOD'S WILL:

Behold, I stand at the door, and knock: If any man hear my voice, and open the door, I will come in to him, and will sup with him, and he with me."

Revelations 3:20

That door is the door of your heart, and the person is **JESUS CHRIST**! He *alone* can fill the void, the empty place in your life. He died to pay the penalty for your sins, but He also rose from the dead to give you life and reunite you with God. This personal relationship with Jesus is the only thing that can fill your need, because that is what your need really *is*. It's simple — just admit that you're a sinner, and ask Jesus to forgive you. Ask Jesus to come into your heart and life and to be your Lord and Savior. Confess with your mouth, believe in your heart, and you shall be saved.

GOD'S WILL:
That if thou shalt confess with thy mouth the Lord Jesus, and shalt believe in thine heart that God hath raised him from the dead, thou shalt be saved. For with the heart man believeth unto righteousness; and with the mouth confession is made unto salvation.
Romans 10: 9-10

MY DECISION

Being convinced that I am a lost sinner, I now believe that Christ died for me so God could forgive my sins. I have now received the Lord Jesus Christ as my personal Savior. Jesus has filled the void, the gap, the empty place in me on this day _____,
I now sign my name committing my life to Jesus.

Name_____

We would like to share in your celebration.

Please send your decision to:

Step by Step Ministries
Jim and Carla Barbarossa
215 Sauk Trail • Valparaiso, IN 46385
or call 219-762-7589
E-mail: stepbystep@step-by-step.org
website: step-by-step.org

CHAPTER 3
The Birthing of Equipping the Saints For the Work of the Ministry

In October 1996, Jim and Carla went to Kenya as the worship leaders for another ministry. When they got there, they saw hundreds of posters on every building and telephone pole. To their amazement, they were listed as speakers for a healing crusade.

GOD'S WILL:
And he said unto them, Go ye into all the world, and preach the gospel to every creature.
Mark 16:15

Totally unprepared, Jim and Carla were split off from the group. It was at this point that God gave them four messages on equipping the saints for the work of the ministry. During one of the meetings, it was prophesied that Jim and Carla would not see the fruit of these meetings until they got home. After they got home, the good reports came forth.

GOD'S WILL:

Howbeit when he, the Spirit of truth, is come, he will guide you into all truth: for he shall not speak of himself; but whatsoever he shall hear, that shall he speak: and he will shew you things to come. He shall glorify me: for he shall receive of mine, and shall shew it unto you.

John 16: 13-14

GOD'S WILL:

But the anointing which ye have received of him abideth in you, and ye need not that any man teach you: but as the same anointing teacheth you of all things, and is truth, and is no lie, and even as it hath taught you, ye shall abide in him.

1 John 2:27

Jim and Carla made themselves available and God filled their mouths by the Holy Spirit.

Have you made yourself available to God?

GOOD REPORTS:

Pastor Moses: *"My people are excited; they are hearing things that they can relate to and practically apply to their own lives! They can't wait to come back tomorrow."*

Pastor Jackson: *"I have already had people tell me, Pastor, I have not been obedient to God's voice. I know I need to make changes. I need to do what God tells me. Jim and Carla, do you know what God is doing here through you? God is equipping the Saints for the work of the ministry."*

GOD'S WILL:
And he gave some, apostles; and some,
prophets; and some, evangelists; and
some, pastors and teachers; For the per-
fecting of the saints, for the work of the
ministry, for the edifying of the body of
Christ:

Ephesians 4: 11-12

Bro. George: *"We give Glory to God for the message He put in your heart for us. It brought deliverance! Healing! And has set the captives free. The church of God has been highly uplifted."*

Pastor Solomon: *"Just to mention the fruits of your labor, there was a woman with a limb problem and her, daughter was paralyzed. After you had prayed for her, you told her to go home and lay her hands on her daughter. As she prayed, the miracle of healing met them. The daughter came on Saturday to church for worship just after you departed. She was saved! And won! She continues well. Belonging to God! Amen!"*

GOD'S WILL:
And they went forth, and preached every
where, the Lord working with them, and
confirming the word with signs following.
Amen.

Mark 16:20

Rev. Ongero: *"There were two notable healing miracles that God did in those meetings."*
1. *"There was a woman of about sixty five who came to the meeting who had been sick for many years. She had been in the hospital. You prayed for her to receive healing. Instantly she received her healing. She*

doubted her healing so she did not say anything that night. She went home and slept nicely without pain. She realized that God had touched her on Friday. She came with a powerful testimony, which excited everybody in the church."

2. *"Another miracle. After this woman received the miracle of healing, she went to her neighbor and testified to her what the Lord had done in the meeting after prayer. That neighbor had a daughter who was admitted in the hospital and was seriously sick. That neighbor came to the meeting on Tuesday. You prayed for her and directed her to go and touch her sick daughter, who could neither walk nor sit. She left the meeting; she went directly to the hospital and touched her daughter & instantly her closed throat and ears were opened! After two days she gained strength and came to church with a powerful testimony and gave Glory to the Lord."*

GOD'S WILL:
> **And these signs shall follow them that believe; In my name shall they cast out devils; they shall speak with new tongues; they shall take up serpents; and if they drink any deadly thing, it shall not hurt them; they shall lay hands on the sick, and they shall recover.**
> **Mark 16: 17-18**

These Christians believed and signs followed. God gave Jim and Carla messages to equip the saints. The saints believed and went forth doing the work of the ministry.

GOD'S WILL:

So shall my word be that goeth forth out of my mouth: it shall not return unto me void, but it shall accomplish that which I please, and it shall prosper in the thing whereto I sent it.

Isaiah 55:11

God provided these messages by His Spirit. They were God's Word and they did not come back void. They went forth and prospered where they were sent.

Since the birthing of the Equipping the Saints series in Kenya, Africa, Jim and Carla have been teaching it all across the USA and around the world.

The "Equipping the Saints" series is available on audiocassette tape. See Item No. 2 on order form in back of book.

CHAPTER 4
The Trumpet
Has Sounded
— Repent!

A cry for repentance is going forth. Repent! Repent!

GOD'S WILL:
Cry aloud, spare not, lift up thy voice like a trumpet, and shew my people their transgression, and the house of Jacob their sins.

Isaiah 58:1

Sin must be recognized (admitted to) and confessed as sin.

What Sin?
The Sin of Disobedience!

What Sin?
The Sin of Not Obeying the Great Commission!

What Sin?
The Sin of Not Being a Witness for Jesus!

What Sin?
The Sin of Not Being a Minister of Reconciliation!

What does *Reconciliation* mean? Let me show you!

GOD'S WILL:

Therefore if any man be in Christ, he is a new creature: old things are passed away; behold, all things are become new.

2 Corinthians 5:17

If you are in Christ; if you know Jesus as Savior, these verses are talking about you.

GOD'S WILL:

And all things are of God, who hath reconciled us to himself by Jesus Christ, and hath given to us the ministry of reconciliation;

2 Corinthians 5:18

Reconcile means:

1. To make compatible with

2. To return to harmony with

3. To take what was once one, that is now split apart and bring it back together

GOD'S WILL:

And God said, Let us make man in our image, after our likeness: and let them have dominion over the fish of the sea, and over the fowl of the air, and over the cattle, and over all the earth, and over every creeping thing that creepeth upon the earth. So God created man in his own image, in the image of God created he him; male and female created he them.

Genesis 1:26-27

GOD'S WILL:

And the Lord God took the man, and put him into the garden of Eden to dress it and to keep it. And the Lord God commanded the man, saying, Of every tree of the garden thou mayest freely eat: but of the tree of the knowledge of good and evil, thou shalt not eat of it: for in the day that thou eatest thereof thou shalt surely die.

Genesis 2:15-17

God placed man in the garden of Eden and told man he could have anything in the garden to eat except of the tree of the knowledge of good and evil.

GOD'S WILL:

And when the woman saw that the tree was good for food, and that it was pleasant to the eyes, and a tree to be desired to make one wise, she took of the fruit thereof, and did eat, and gave also unto her husband with her; and he did eat.

Genesis 3:6

Man ate of the forbidden tree. Man was disobedient to God.

GOD'S WILL:

Therefore the Lord God sent him forth from the garden of Eden, to till the ground from whence he was taken. So he drove out the man; and he placed at the east of the garden of Eden Cherubims, and a flaming sword which turned every way, to keep the way of the tree of life.

Genesis 3: 23-24

Man was separated from God.

GOD'S WILL:
For God so loved the world, that he gave his only begotten Son, that whosoever believeth in him should not perish, but have everlasting life.

John 3:16

God sent His Son, Jesus Christ. He gave His life, dying on the cross, so *all* men could come back into fellowship with God.

THAT IS RECONCILIATION

Jesus died so man could be made *compatible* with God. Jesus died so man could be in *harmony* with God. Can you give me an Amen? Most Christians have no problem saying Amen to this fact!

GOD'S WILL:
And all things are of God, who hath reconciled us to himself by Jesus Christ,

2 Corinthians 5:18A

Now let's look at the rest of the truth in this scripture.

GOD'S WILL:
and hath given to us the ministry of reconciliation;

2 Corinthians 5:18B

TO US!

Who's US?

EVERY PERSON THAT IS SAVED!
Every person that calls Jesus their Savior.

What has Jesus given US?

The ministry of *Reconciliation*!

Remember: Reconciliation means to bring into *harmony*, to make *compatible*, to reunite something that has been separated.

Remember! Man was separated from God & Jesus brought them back together. EVERY person that is born again is to be like Jesus & take sinful men & lead them to God by telling them what Jesus did for them when He died on the cross.

This is usually where the Amens STOP. What do you mean? Well, I bring this message in front of people and this is the place it gets very, very QUIET! AS IN OUCH! Let's continue:

GOD'S WILL:
To wit, that God was in Christ, reconciling the world unto himself, not imputing their trespasses unto them; and hath committed unto us the word of reconciliation.
2 Corinthians 5:19

And hath committed unto us THE WORD of Reconciliation! US! Who's *US*? You and me and all that know Jesus. Committed unto *US* THE WORD of Reconciliation. THE WORD! Words are something we speak. We must speak the TRUTH. We must speak that Jesus died so all men can come back to God. Jesus gave *US* the ministry of reconciliation in verse 18 & then gave *US* the word of reconciliation in verse 19. He told *US* **TWO TIMES.** Now let's look at verse 20.

GOD'S WILL:
Now then we are ambassadors for Christ, as though God did beseech you by us: we pray you in Christ's stead, be ye reconciled to God.
2 Corinthians 5:20

What is an ambassador? An ambasador is a diplomat, a representative, one that goes in the place of another. Jesus came as a Representative of God. Now then WE are ambassadors FOR CHRIST! We (you & I), all that know Jesus as Savior, are called to be representatives for Christ and ambassadors for God.

GOD'S WILL:
> **Now then we are ambassadors for Christ, as though God did beseech you by us: we pray you in Christ's stead, be ye reconciled to God.**
>
> **2 Corinthians 5:20**

We *all* need to be telling the world the last part of verse 20. We pray you, we beg you, sinful man, come to God through Jesus Christ. We need to be shouting this from the roof tops. We need to be shouting this out in the streets where people are lost. Why is it that we have a lot more shouters in the church than we do out in the *world*?

GOD'S WILL:
> **Let the redeemed of the Lord <u>say</u> so, whom he hath redeemed from the hand of the enemy;**
>
> **Psalms 107:2**

Who's the redeemed? All that have been delivered from sin; all that Jesus exchanged His life for; all that Jesus purchased with His blood.

GOD'S WILL:
> **Let the redeemed of the Lord <u>say</u> so, whom he hath redeemed from the hand of the enemy;**
>
> **Psalms 107:2**

"Say so!" What's that mean? To say so is to *BRAG!* To *BOAST!* To *CERTIFY!* To *TELL!* To *DECLARE!* To *SPEAK!* To *ANNOUNCE PUBLICLY!* The bottom line is that all the people whom Jesus died for are to shout, boast, declare, and announce publicly that Jesus has delivered them from DEATH. Can you give me an Amen? The ministry of reconciliation is *not* just for the pastor, evangelist, teacher, prophet or apostle.

GOD'S WILL:
>**Therefore if any man be in Christ, he is a new creature: old things are passed away; behold, all things are become new. And all things are of God, who hath reconciled us to himself by Jesus Christ, _and hath given to us the ministry of reconciliation._**
>**2 Corinthians 5:17-18**

I don't see the words pastor, evangelist, apostle, prophet or teacher anywhere in this Scripture. I have heard plenty people say it's the pastor's job, it's the evangelist's job to witness, to lead the lost to Jesus. THAT'S A LIE! People use this lie to try and justify their disobedience. DISOBEDIENCE IS A SIN! Surveys have shown that 90 to 95% of born again Christians have NEVER led a lost soul to Jesus. THAT'S A LOT OF DISOBEDIENCE. THAT'S A LOT OF SIN! What do you mean, *"Sin?"*

GOD'S WILL:
>**For rebellion is as the sin of witchcraft, and stubbornness is as iniquity and idolatry. Because thou hast rejected the word of the Lord, he hath also rejected thee from being king.**
>**I Samuel 15:23**

For rebellion *(disobedience)* is as the sin of witchcraft. Rebellion is disobedience. Disobedience is sin.

God has given us these commands:

GOD'S WILL:
And Jesus came and spake unto them, saying, All power is given unto me in heaven and in earth. Go ye therefore, and teach all nations, baptizing them in the name of the Father, and of the Son, and of the Holy Ghost: Teaching them to observe all things whatsoever I have commanded you: and, lo, I am with you alway, even unto the end of the world. Amen.

Matthew 28: 18-20

As you go, everywhere you go, teach people, tell people about Jesus.

GOD'S WILL:
And he said unto them, go ye into all the world, and preach the gospel to every creature.

Mark 16:15

Go ye . . . go to your neighbors house, to the people you meet along your daily walk and tell them about Jesus. Demonstrate God's power to them!

GOD'S WILL:
But ye shall receive power, after that the Holy Ghost is come upon you: and ye shall be witnesses unto me both in Jerusalem, and in all Judæa, and in Samaria, and unto the uttermost part of the earth.

Acts 1:8

We are to be a witness for Jesus in near places, far away places, in every place, to every people. Have you accepted your part as a minister of reconciliation? Do you live like it? Have you accepted your part in the great commission? Are you living like it? Are you being a witness for Jesus? Are the members of your local church living like ministers of reconciliation? Are the members of your local church living a great commission lifestyle? Remember the statistics say 90% to 95% of all born again Christians have never led a lost person to Jesus. THAT'S A LOT OF SIN! THAT'S A LOT OF UNCONFESSED SIN!

GOD'S WILL:
Behold, the Lord's hand is not shortened, that it cannot save; neither his ear heavy, that it cannot hear: But your iniquities have separated between you and your God, and your sins have hid his face from you, that he will not hear.
Isaiah 59: 1-2

If we don't call sin - sin, if we don't admit to it and confess it, we will separate ourselves from God. THE TRUMPET HAS SOUNDED . . . REPENT!

GOD'S WILL:
Cry aloud, spare not, lift up thy voice like a trumpet, and shew my people their transgression, and the house of Jacob their sins.
Isaiah 58:1

REPENT! My friends, this is a hard message. It is the truth. It is the gospel. It's not going to change. It's not going away. It's part of God's Word. It will last forever.

This truth needs to be preached in every church everywhere. God's calling for repentance and change. THE END IS COMING SOON! THE TRUMPET HAS SOUNDED . . . REPENT!

GOD'S WILL:
Blow ye the trumpet in Zion, and sound an alarm in my holy mountain: let all the inhabitants of the land tremble: for the day of the Lord cometh, for it is nigh at hand;
Joel 2:1

"For the day of the Lord cometh, for it is nigh at hand!"

GOD'S WILL:
Therefore also now, saith the Lord, turn ye even to me with all your heart, and with fasting, and with weeping and with mourning: And rend your heart and not your garments, and turn unto the Lord your God: for he is gracious and merciful, slow to anger, and of great kindness, and repenteth him of the evil.
Joel 2:12-13

Repent! Turn to God! Change!

GOD'S WILL:
Come now, and let us reason together, saith the Lord: though your sins be as scarlet, they shall be as white as snow; though they be red like crimson, they shall be as wool. If ye be willing and obedient, ye shall eat the good of the land: But if ye refuse and rebel, ye shall be devoured with

the sword: for the mouth of the Lord hath spoken it.

Isaiah 1:18 to 20

It's time to be willing and obedient!

Read these Quotes[1]:

"We need to stop condemning sinners for not coming to church to hear the gospel and start condemning Christians for not going from the church with the gospel."

Freddie Gage

"The greatest strike of our generation has not been by Labor Unions, but by twentieth century Christians, the Army of God which has refused to follow the Savior's commands."

Billy Graham

"There are two kinds of Christians, soul winners and backsliders."

Andrew Murray

"The Trumpet Has Sounded, Repent"
is available on videotape.
See Item No. 3 on order form in back of book.

[1]Quotes from book, "Go Tell" by Freddie Gage, Pages 4, 5, & 19.

A VOICE FROM ETERNITY

You lived next door to me for years;
We shared our dreams, our joys, our tears.
A friend to me you were indeed -
A friend who helped me when in need.
My faith in you was strong and sure;
We had such trust as should endure.
No spats between us ever rose;
Our friends were alike, also our foes.
What sadness, then, my friend, to find
That after all, you weren't so kind.
The day my life on earth did end,
I found you weren't a faithful friend.
For all those years we spent on earth,
you never talked of the second birth,
And of the Christ who'd make me whole.
I plead today from hell's cruel fire
And tell you now my last desire:
You cannot do a thing for me,
No words today my bonds will free.
But do not err, my friend, again,
Do all you can for souls of men.
Plead with them now quite earnestly
Lest they be cast in hell with me.

Author Unknown
Luke 16:19-31, Matthew 8:12,
Revelation 14:9-12, 20:10

Could this be your neighbor?

Could this be you?

CHAPTER 5
Jesus
Gave Gifts

Jesus gave Gifts.

GOD'S WILL:
   Wherefore he saith, When he ascended up on high, he led captivity captive, and gave gifts unto men.
                                          Ephesians 4:8

In other words: Jesus arose from the grave and went to Heaven. Jesus then took all that He was and poured Himself into gifts.

What Gifts?

GOD'S WILL:
   And he gave some, apostles; and some, prophets; and some, evangelists; and some, pastors and teachers;
                                          Ephesians 4:11

In other words: He gave gifts of apostles, prophets, evangelists, pastors and teachers.

Why did he give these gifts?

GOD'S WILL:
For the perfecting of the saints, for the work of the ministry, for the edifying of the body of Christ.

Ephesians 4:12

In other words: Jesus gave these gifts to men *(to the church)* so that the saints *(all Christians, all that call Jesus Savior)* can be perfected *(matured, equipped)* to do the work of the ministry. Simply put, to learn how to do what Jesus did. To be a servant like Jesus. To edify *(build up)* the body of Christ.

Jesus gave of what He was!

GOD'S WILL:
Wherefore, holy brethren, partakers of the heavenly calling, consider the Apostle and High Priest of our profession, Christ Jesus;

Hebrews 3:1

JESUS the APOSTLE

GOD'S WILL:
And they were offended in him. But Jesus said unto them, A prophet is not without honour, save in his own country, and in his own house.

Matthew 13:57

JESUS the PROPHET

GOD'S WILL:

For the son of a man is come to seek and
to save that which was lost.

Luke 19:10

JESUS the EVANGELIST

GOD'S WILL:

I am the good shepherd: the good shepherd giveth his life for the sheep. But he
that is an hireling, and not the shepherd,
whose own the sheep are not, seeth the
wolf coming, and leaveth the sheep, and
fleeth: and the wolf catcheth them, and
scattereth the sheep. The hireling fleeth,
because he is an hireling, and careth not
for the sheep. I am the good shepherd,
and know my sheep, and am known of
mine.

John 10:11-14

JESUS the PASTOR

GOD'S WILL:

And Jesus went about all the cities and
villages, teaching in their synagogues, and
preaching the gospel of the kingdom, and
healing every sickness and every disease
among the people.

Matthew 9:35

JESUS the TEACHER

GOD'S WILL:

For he whom God has sent speaketh the words of God: for God giveth not the Spirit by measure unto him. The Father loveth the Son, and hath given all things into his hand.

John 3:34-35

Jesus had the Spirit without measure.

Jesus had the fullness of the anointing.

So, Jesus took all that He was, the fullness of the Anointing, the Spirit without measure and poured Himself out, and all that He was, out into the five gifts that he gave the church.

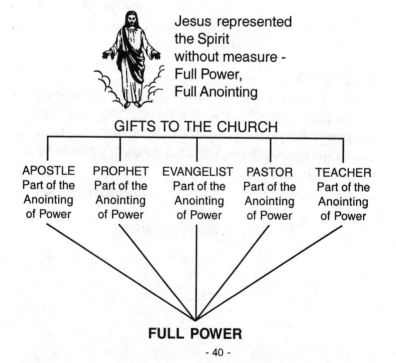

Jesus represented the Spirit without measure - Full Power, Full Anointing

GIFTS TO THE CHURCH

APOSTLE	PROPHET	EVANGELIST	PASTOR	TEACHER
Part of the Anointing of Power	Part of the Anointing of Power	Part of the Anointing of Power	Part of the Anointing of Power	Part of the Anointing of Power

FULL POWER

All five-Ministry Gifts must function together for the church to have the fullness of the Power, and the Fullness of the Anointing of Jesus.

Let's look at this example:

You're going down the road in your 5-cylinder engine car. One cylinder stops running! What happens?

YOU LOSE POWER!

You need all 5-cylinders for your car to have full power.

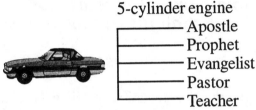

5-cylinder engine
— Apostle
— Prophet
— Evangelist
— Pastor
— Teacher

Let's say that this car is the church and its 5-cylinder engine represents the five gifts Jesus gave the church.

How can you get your car to move at full power?

That's simple! Use all the gifts Jesus has given the body. Use all five cylinders. Have you ever wondered why there is a lack of power in the church today? Could it be that we have limited God's power by limiting the use of the five gifts Christ gave the church?

How many gifts did Jesus give to perfect the Saints?

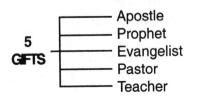

5 GIFTS
— Apostle
— Prophet
— Evangelist
— Pastor
— Teacher

If we are not using all five-gifts, can we ever expect the saints to be brought to maturity?

Do you think Jesus gave five-gifts for a reason?

Do you think we should use them all?

GOD'S WILL:
For my thoughts are not your thoughts, neither are your ways my ways, saith the Lord. For as the heavens are higher than the earth, so are my ways higher than your ways, and my thoughts than your thoughts.

Isaiah 55:8-9

Maybe it's time we do it Jesus' way. His ways are higher than ours!

Jesus knew exactly what He was doing when He gave five gifts to the church.

If we want to see the saints truly equipped to do the work of the ministry, we must use all five gifts that Jesus has given us. How many cylinders are powering your local church?

Place a check in the box of each gift that functions in your church. How can we cry out to God for more power, and anointing, when we won't use the gifts He has given us to perfect and mature us?

❑ Apostle
❑ Prophet
❑ Evangelist
❑ Pastor
❑ Teacher

Pray! Seek God as to His will for your local church concerning the use of the five gifts that Jesus gave the church.

Jesus Gave Gifts
Video Series

A Teaching on the Five-Fold Ministry
Based on Ephesians 4:11 & 12

GOD'S WILL:
And he gave some, apostles; and some, prophets; and some, evangelists; and some, pastors and teachers; For the perfecting of the saints, for the work of the ministry, for the edifying of the body of Christ:

Ephesians 4:11-12

This video series is a great tool for classroom settings, leadership seminars, Christian colleges, schools of higher education, Bible studies and the local church to help raise up strong Christian leaders. It is an in-depth study of the five gifts Jesus gave the church. A must for anyone that God has called into the Five Fold Ministry.

See Item No. 4 on order form in back of book.

Evangelist Come Forth

CHAPTER 6
The Gift of the Evangelist
Part 1

The word EVANGELIST appears only three places in the scripture. Let's look at them.

The First Place:

GOD'S WILL:
But watch thou in all things, endure af-flictions, do the work of an evangelist, make full proof of thy ministry.
2 Timothy 4:5

In this verse, Apostle Paul is telling Timothy to do the work of an evangelist. When I read that, it brings up the question, what is the work of an evangelist?

The Second Place:

GOD'S WILL:
And the next day we that were of Paul's company departed, and came unto Caesarea: and we entered into the house

of Philip the evangelist, which was one of the seven; and abode with him.

Acts 21:8

So we see that Philip was an evangelist and was one of the seven, and that prompts another question in my mind. One of what seven?

GOD'S WILL:
Wherefore, brethren, look ye out among you seven men of honest report, full of the Holy Ghost and wisdom, whom we may appoint over this business. But we will give ourselves continually to prayer, and to the ministry of the Word. And the saying pleased the whole multitude: and they chose Stephen, a man full of faith and of the Holy Ghost, and Philip and Prochorus, and Nicanor, and Timon, and Parmenas, and Nicolas a proselyte of Antioch:

Acts 6:3-5

We know that Philip was an evangelist; we know that he was one of the seven. We also know that Philip was submitted to and was under the authority of the Jerusalem Church. Let's look at that same Philip two chapters later to see what this evangelist does.

GOD'S WILL:
Then Philip went down to the city of Samaria, and preached Christ unto them.

Acts 8:5

Philip went to Samaria and preached the good news to them. He preached Jesus Christ to them.

GOD'S WILL:

And the people with one accord gave heed unto those things which Philip spake, hearing and seeing the miracles which he did.

Acts 8:6

When Christ was preached, the people listened and received what was said and miracles followed the preaching of the Word.

GOD'S WILL:

For unclean spirits, crying with loud voice, came out of many that were possessed with them; and many taken with palsies, and that were lame, were healed.

Acts 8:7

As Philip the evangelist ministered, captives were set free and sick were healed.

GOD'S WILL:

But when they believed Philip preaching the things concerning the kingdom of God, and the name of Jesus Christ, they were baptized, both men and women.

Acts 8:12

They believed; they were born again! They were saved.

GOD'S WILL:

Now when the apostles which were at Jerusalem heard that Samaria had received the word of God, they sent unto them Peter and John:

Acts 8:14

Philip worked with the Apostles. Philip was not a lone ranger. Philip worked with the other five fold ministers.

GOD'S WILL:
And the angel of the Lord spake unto Philip, saying, Arise, and go toward the south unto the way that goeth down from Jerusalem unto Gaza, which is desert.
Acts 8:26

When Philip's work was done in Samaria, God directed his steps by an angel. He worked with the church, with the apostles, but his steps were ordered by God.

GOD'S WILL:
And he arose and went: and, behold, a man of Ethiopia, an eunuch of great authority under Candace queen of the Ethiopians, who had the charge of all her treasure, and had come to Jerusalem for to worship, Was returning, and sitting in his chariot read Esaias the prophet.
Acts 8:27-28

When God spoke through the angel, Philip arose and went. He did not seek permission from man. He went as God directed. He worked with the apostles and the church, but he was led by God. An evangelist must be led by the Spirit, but must also be in submission to those God has put in authority over him.

In earlier verses, we read that Philip ministered to many. This time God sent him for one man. A man of great authority, a man that could influence many people. A man that was searching for the truth.

GOD'S WILL:
Then the Spirit said unto Philip, Go near, and join thyself to this chariot. And Philip ran thither to him, and heard him read the prophet Esaias, and said, Understandest thou what thou readest? And he said, How can I, except some man should guide me? And he desired Philip that he would come up and sit with him.

Acts 8:29-31

Again Philip the evangelist was led by the Spirit. Because he obeyed the angel, he was in the place God wanted him, and ready to take the next step. The Spirit led him to a man that was searching for help, a man the Father was drawing. When help arrived, the man welcomed it!

GOD'S WILL:
Then Philip opened his mouth, and began at the same scripture, and preached unto him Jesus.

Acts 8:35

Philip always preached Christ.

GOD'S WILL
And when they were come up out of the water, the Spirit of the Lord caught away Philip, that the eunuch saw him no more: and he went on his way rejoicing.

Acts 8:39

When Philip's work was done here, the Spirit of the Lord took him to his next assignment.

GOD'S WILL:

But Philip was found at Azotus: and passing through he preached in all the cities, till he came to Cæsarea.

Acts 8:40

Philip the evangelist had a call to the lost. He sometimes reached the lost many at a time and sometimes it was one on one. He was moved from place to place by God. He was led by the Holy Spirit and preached Jesus Christ everywhere he went. He was under the authority of God and was also under the authority of the apostles in Jerusalem.

GOD'S WILL:

Wherefore, brethren, look ye out among you seven men of honest report, full of the Holy Ghost and wisdom, whom we may appoint over this business. But we will give ourselves continually to prayer, and to the ministry of the word. And the saying pleased the whole multitude: and they chose Stephen, a man full of faith and of the Holy Ghost, and Philip, and Prochorus, and Nicanor, and Timon, and Parmenas, and Nicolas a proselyte of Antioch: Whom they set before the apostles: and when they had prayed, they laid their hands on them.

Acts 6:3-6

Philip was under the authority of the church in Jerusalem and at the same time led by the Spirit of God. Even though he was submitted to the authority of the Jerusalem church, his movement was not controlled by them. His path was controlled by the Holy Spirit. By humbly subjecting ourselves one to another, I believe we can be submitted to the authority God has over us and at the same time be led by the Holy Spirit.

The Third Place:

GOD'S WILL:
And he gave some, apostles; and some prophets; and some, evangelists; and some, pastors and teachers; For the perfecting of the saints, for the work of the ministry, for the edifying of the body of Christ.
Ephesians 4:11-12

Jesus gave Five-Gifts to the Church *(Apostle, Prophet, Evangelist, Pastor, Teacher)* to perfect the saints to do the work of the ministry.

The Evangelist is one of the Five-Gifts that Jesus gave to the church to perfect the saints.

Who Are The Saints?
Christians! Those That Are Saved!

So, the Evangelist is not only a gift to the lost, but also to the saints. An Evangelist is to help perfect those that have already been saved. An Evangelist is to help stir up those that are saved so they will go out & help others get saved. The Evangelist has two main jobs.

1. Introduce the Lost to Jesus.

2. Teach, train, mature, perfect, equip and activate the Saints *(Christians)* to win the lost for Jesus.

Why is the Evangelist needed in the local church?

Because 90% to 95% of all Christians have never led a lost soul to Jesus. *That's a big need!*

Evangelist Come Forth

CHAPTER 7
The Gift of the Evangelist
Part 2

Do you know what an Evangelist is? Do you know what an Evangelist does? I *THOUGHT* I did. I thought an Evangelist preached a message, gave an invitation and people came forth to be saved. Is that what you thought? Well, that's part of being an Evangelist, but there is more. What's the *more?*

GOD'S WILL:
And he gave some, apostles; and some, prophets; and some, evangelists; and some, pastors and teachers; For the perfecting of the saints, for the work of the ministry, for the edifying of the body of Christ:

Ephesians 4:11-12

Jesus gave five Gifts to the Church *(Apostle, Prophet, Evangelist, Pastor, Teacher)* TO PERFECT THE SAINTS to do the work of the ministry.

The Evangelist is one of the five gifts that Jesus gave to the church to perfect the saints. Who are the Saints? Christians! Those that are saved! So, the Evangelist is not only a gift to the lost, but also to the saints. An Evangelist is to help perfect those that have already been saved. An Evangelist is to help stir up those that are saved so they will go out and help others find salvation.

Statistics say that 90% of all born again believers have NEVER led a lost soul to Jesus! I have found that most Christians do not have the faith to believe that they can lead a lost soul to Jesus. Why is this? Could it be that they have not heard enough messages that would build their faith in this area?

GOD'S WILL:
So then faith cometh by hearing, and hearing by the word of God.
Romans 10:17

If faith comes by hearing and hearing by the Word, as leaders, shouldn't we make it a priority that the saints hear about winning the lost? Shouldn't we do whatever it takes to build their faith to win souls?

My brothers and sisters in Christ, my fellow five-fold ministers, we must make changes; we must focus on the reason God sent Jesus: **SOULS.**

GOD'S WILL:
For God so loved the world, that he gave his only begotten Son, that whosoever believeth in him should not perish, but have everlasting life.
John 3:16

The focus of God's people must be on winning the LOST! The purpose of the Church MUST be reaching the lost!

I believe we can evaluate what our priorities are by how much time we give to things. Look at your local congregation, the part of the body you call home.

How much time is spent teaching the saints to reach the lost? How much time is spent on fellowship dinners? How much time is spent on bake sales? How much time is spent on luncheons? How much time is spent on prosperity messages? How much time is spent on weight loss programs? How much time is spent on choir practice or worship team practice? How much time is spent on church picnics? How much time is spent on prophecy? How much time is spent on concerts? How much time is spent on holidays, events, plays, or programs? These are just a few of the many things that seem to have a HIGHER PRIORITY THAN SOULS!

I believe God is calling the Evangelist to come forth. We need to hear from those that are anointed to stir our hearts towards reaching the lost.

A pastor and I were talking a few months ago and he said to me, *"Jim, I have tried everything I know to stir up my congregation. It's just not working."*

As he shared that with me, I felt prompted by the Lord to say, *"Well, did you ever think that you're having a problem in that area because it's really not your calling. Maybe God has someone else to help you with that part? Maybe you need the gift of the Evangelist?"*

Let me share a testimony with you: In February 1999, we taught at a local church for three services. During the first two services, we taught on soul winning and being a disciple of Jesus. During the third service, the pastor asked for testimonies. Six different people shared how their hearts had been stirred toward souls during the first two services and how during the week they had a heart to focus on the lost. Between those six people they led ten lost souls to Jesus. They did not go door knocking or set out to look for souls. They just reached out to those that God brought near them each day.

YES! We can learn to win the lost.

HOW?

Set priorities.

Make reaching the lost priority number one!

How do I do that? Allow time each week to keep everyone's focus on souls.

Seek God as to who the local Evangelist is for your church. When God shows you, give them five to eight minutes every **Sunday morning** to bring a mini-sermon to encourage soul winning. *(Do this before you dismiss the youth and children. They need to hear these type of messages to mold them & build their faith. Remember faith comes by hearing.)* When you start doing this, the first thing that will happen is EVERYTHING WILL HAPPEN. You will be hit with a hundred reasons each service why you should save some time and cancel the five to eight minutes for Evangelism. The devil does not want you keeping people's focus on lost souls.

I was given the honor of bringing short messages each week in our local church and every week, some problem came up to try and cancel that message.

Set your focus; make that focus lost souls. If nothing else gets done during a service, set your priority that the saints will be reminded about the lost and equipped to go out and reach them.

Jesus gave five gifts to the church; they each have a different part to do to equip the saints. Each gift has an anointing to do different things.

A teacher may have the anointing to impart knowledge, but may not be able to ACTIVATE people to use that knowledge.

We have a lot of great teachers in the Body of Christ, Christians probably have more knowledge than ever. But nine out of ten still never tell the lost about Jesus. Teaching in itself is not enough. God's people must be activated, motivated, stirred up, and prompted to use all the teaching they have received to *win the lost.*

EVANGELIST COME FORTH!

God is calling forth Evangelists to work with the saints to teach them how to reach the lost. Please join us in praying for those that Jesus has called to be Evangelists to the local church — to stand up and accept their commission. Also pray that those people Jesus has called as Evangelists will be recognized, accepted and openly received into the part of the body where God wants them.

GOD'S WILL:
And he gave some, apostles; and some, prophets; and some, evangelists; and some, pastors and teachers; For the perfecting of the saints, for the work of the ministry, for the edifying of the body of Christ:
Ephesians 4:11-12

Remember, the Word of God says Jesus gave the Evangelist for the perfecting of the saints. To work with Christians. What better place can there be than the local church for an Evangelist to work with the saints?

EVANGELIST COME FORTH NOW!

Souls are counting on you.

"The Gift of the Evangelist"
is available on videotape. See Item No. 5 on order
form in back of book.

CHAPTER 8
God Wants To Use
Your Testimony
Part 1

God wants to use your testimony!
YES! Your testimony!

Not your neighbor's, not someone else's. God wants
to use your testimony. God will anoint your testimony.

GOD'S WILL:
**And they overcame him by the blood of
the Lamb, and by the word of their testimony; and they loved not their lives unto
the death.**
Revelations 12:11

The *"him"* is satan. The overcoming by the blood of
the Lamb is what Jesus did when He died on the cross
and arose from the dead to defeat satan. "By the word of
their testimony" — that's YOUR part.

"My part?"

"Yes, your part!" When was the last time you told a
lost soul what Jesus has done for you?

If you know Jesus as Savior, you have a testimony.
Your testimony can be a powerful tool for reaching the
lost. What is a testimony? A testimony should have three
parts:

1. My life before I knew Jesus.

2. How I got to know Jesus.

3. How Jesus has changed my life.

That's all there is to it. Sharing a testimony is telling a lost person what you were like before you knew Jesus, how you met Jesus, and how Jesus has changed your life. Your testimony of Jesus should very plainly tell people what Jesus has done for you and what Jesus will do for them. Your testimony can be a powerful tool to reach people who already know you. Will you allow God to use your testimony to reach a lost soul? Will you? It's not hard. Actually it's very easy!

"How can I get started?"

Here's how:

1. Write down on a piece of paper what your life was like before you met Jesus.

2. Write down how you met Jesus.

3. Write down how Jesus changed your life.

4. Write a prayer so the person reading your testimony can ask Jesus to forgive them and come into their heart.

5. Invite the person reading to come and fellowship with you. Give your name, and your church's name, address and phone number.

If you would like a few sample testimonies, call or write and we will send them to you.

Let me tell you what happened the first time I sent out my written testimony. I sent it to a man who had rented a house from me.

A week after I sent it, his wife called and said, *"I want to thank you so much for sending your testimony to my husband."* He read it and said, "If God could change Jim like that, maybe He can change me."

About a week or so later, I saw this man coming down my driveway. I knew who it was, but he looked different. It was the man I had sent the testimony to. When he got up to my door, he told me that he was saved that Sunday. Praise God! He also said that three other members of his family were saved that same day. Thank you Jesus.

The testimony I sent was worth about two pennies, the cost of a piece of paper, (Pretty much worthless, or of little or no value). But oh, what God can do with a piece of paper! What the anointing of God can do with a piece of paper! What the anointing of God can do to the person reading that piece of paper!

God did it. God anointed the testimony but it took a willing person to write and give that testimony to someone so God could use it for His purposes.

Will you let God use
your testimony for His Glory?

GOD'S WILL:
And they overcame him by the blood of the Lamb, and by the word of their testimony; and they loved not their lives unto the death.
Revelations 12:11

"And they loved not their lives unto death." And they were willing to share what Jesus had done for them no matter what the cost. How about you? Are you willing to risk that someone may get mad at you? Are you willing to risk that the person you give your testimony to may reject it? And if they do, you must remember they are not rejecting YOU; they are rejecting JESUS.

Fear and pride stop many Christians from sharing their testimonies. If they have stopped you, repent and seek God's help and take authority over them. Fear and pride are not of God. If you need prayer support in breaking the strongholds of fear and pride, call us and we will help you break these bondages in Jesus' name.

God anoints paper and sends His power
through the hands of a man.

One day the Lord led me to give a man a couple of written testimonies and a small Red Tract Bible. Three months passed and I saw the man one day and he said, "You know I go to church now. Do you remember those testimonies you gave me? I put them on my desk and a couple of weeks ago I just felt I had to pick up that little red bible." He said, "When I did, something went through my hands. I never felt anything like that before. My wife told me the only time she ever felt anything like that was in church. I was saved and baptized."

The power of the Holy Spirit went through the man's hands. If you will share your testimony to God's Glory, God will anoint it.

On another occasion, I gave my testimony to a clerk in a bank. A week later my wife went to the bank. The lady I gave it to thanked my wife for me giving it to her. She said to my wife, *"You know that void or emptiness your husband had, I have that too. Do you think I could go to church with you?"* We visited her house a few days later and prayed with her.

Again, it was just a piece of paper. But oh, what God can do with a piece of paper. God did it, but He needed someone to write their testimony and give it to a lost soul so He could save them. Are you ready to share your testimony to God's Glory? If you will give them out, God will touch people through them! God will anoint your testimony!

The following are just a few ways to share your written testimony:

1. Give one to every person you know . . . friends, family, co-worker, neighbors.

2. When paying bills, insert them with your payment . . . phone bill, water bill, gas bill, light

bill, car payment, house payment. Just imagine somebody is working and they open your payment and receive Jesus! *Praise God!*

3. Send one to every member of your high school graduating class.

4. When you eat out, leave one along with your tip.

5. When you stay in a hotel, leave one along with a tip for the person that cleans your room.

6. Send one to every person on your Christmas mailing list.

7. As you go through your daily duties, keep one handy to give to anyone the Holy Spirit may lead you to. Keep a stash in your car.

8. Send one to people you do business with . . . barber, hair dresser, doctor, lawyer, accountant.

9. Send one to your Public Officials.

10. Keep open for every opportunity. Example, a young boy lost his baseball glove; and our son found it. We called the phone number that was written in the glove. His mother picked up the glove and we gave her a copy of our testimony.

11. Business owners . . . give a testimony to every customer.

God wants to use your testimony!
Will you allow Him to?

Souls are counting on you!

CHAPTER 9
God Wants
To Use
Your Testimony
Part 2

GOD'S WILL:
And they overcame him by the blood of the Lamb, and by the word of their testimony; and they loved not their lives unto the death.

Revelations 12:11

The *"him"* is satan. The overcoming by the blood of the Lamb is what Jesus did when He died on the cross and arose from the dead to defeat satan. "By the word of their testimony," that's YOUR part.

GOD'S WILL:
O give thanks unto the Lord, for he is good: for his mercy endureth for ever. Let the redeemed of the Lord say so, whom he hath redeemed from the hand of the enemy;

Psalm 107:1-2

Redeem means, to deliver from sin, to pay off, to purchase, to exchange, to take one's place. Who is the Redeemer? The one that paid the price for the redeemed. What was that price? His life! His blood! His resurrection! Who is the Redeemer? JESUS.

Jesus died for the sins of all people. Who are the redeemed? Those that have received forgiveness of sin by accepting Jesus Christ and the work that He did when He shed His blood on the cross for them.

GOD'S WILL:
Let the redeemed of the Lord say so, whom he hath redeemed from the hand of the enemy;

Psalms 107:2

Say so? What does that mean?

To say so is to brag, boast, certify, declare, publish, tell, speak or announce publicly. So what's it mean for the redeemed of the Lord to say so?

Let the Redeemed *(those delivered from sin, bought with the price of Jesus' blood, Christians)* say so, let them *(brag, boast, certify, declare, publish, tell, speak, or announce publicly)* how Jesus has set them free from the hand of satan. The Redeemed *(Christians)* are to share the WORD OF THEIR TESTIMONY with those that are lost, so they, too, will have the chance of being redeemed.

When is the last time you shared your testimony with a lost person? When was the last time you bragged or boasted to a lost person about Jesus and what He has done for you?

So what does it mean, let the redeemed of the Lord say so? I like to say it this way! It means, to shout from the roof tops that this is my Jesus; this is what Jesus has done for me and this is what Jesus will do for you. Come and meet Jesus.

How often should we share our testimony to God's Glory?

GOD'S WILL:
I have set watchmen upon thy walls, O Jerusalem, which shall never hold their peace day nor night: ye that make mention of the Lord, keep not silence,
Isaiah 62:6

Unceasingly all the time.

*How often should we be ready
to share our testimony to God's Glory?*

GOD'S WILL:
But sanctify the Lord God in your hearts: and be ready always to give an answer to every man that asketh you a reason of the hope that is in you with meekness and fear:
I Peter 3:15

Always be ready. Be constantly ready.

*Are you ready to share the hope that is in you
with the people God brings into your life today?*

*Should we share our testimony about
the Blessings God has given us?*

GOD'S WILL:
I will mention the loving-kindnesses of the Lord, and the praises of the Lord, according to all that the Lord hath bestowed on us, and the great goodness toward the house of Israel, which he hath bestowed on them according to his mercies, and according to the multitude of his lovingkindnesses.
Isaiah 63:7

YES! We should always take every opportunity to brag on what God has done and will do.

Should my testimony be irrepressible?

GOD'S WILL:
For we cannot but speak the things which we have seen and heard.

Acts 4:20

Yes! Your testimony should be irrepressible!

The world should not be able to stop it. You should not be able to contain it. You should not be able to hold it in. It should come forth like a flood! It should come forth like a river of life and touch all that are around you. God did not save you just for you. You have been saved to help others get saved. Your testimony of Jesus should flow freely from your lips. You should be infectious. You should be using your testimony to infect others with the Gospel of Jesus Christ.

Should I share my testimony to God's Glory?

GOD'S WILL:
Declare his glory among the heathen, his wonders among all people.

Psalms 96:3

YES! You should share your testimony to his glory among the lost and His miracles among all people.

Did Jesus ever say to share a testimony?

GOD'S WILL:
And when he was come into the ship, he that had been possessed with the devil prayed him that he might be with him.

> *Howbeit Jesus suffered him not, but saith unto him, Go home to thy friends, and tell them how great things the Lord hath done for thee, and hath had compassion on thee.*
> *Mark 5:18-19*

Jesus said go tell your family and friends the testimony of how I set you free. Do you think Jesus is still telling those that He has set free to go home and tell their family & friends? ABSOLUTELY. His message has not changed. *"Go Tell."* Have you been set free? Has Jesus delivered you from the hand of satan? Have you told anybody? Have you used your testimony to reach a lost person?

Are you embarassed to share your testimony?

GOD'S WILL:
> *Be not thou therefore ashamed of the testimony of our Lord, nor of me his prisoner: but be thou partaker of the afflictions of the gospel according to the power of God;*
> *2 Timothy 1:8*

Be Not Ashamed!

What did David say about giving testimonies?

GOD'S WILL:
> *That I may publish with the voice of thanksgiving, and tell of all thy wondrous works.*
> *Psalms 26:7*

David was saying that he would testify, that he would tell people about all the great works that he has seen God do.

GOD'S WILL:
**All thy works shall praise thee, O Lord;
and thy saints shall bless thee. They shall
speak of the glory of thy kingdom, and
talk of thy power; To make known to the
sons of men his mighty acts, and the glo-
rious majesty of his kingdom.**
Psalms 145:10-12

Saints are to testify, to speak, to talk of God's glory
and power to the sons of men *(the lost)*.

GOD'S WILL:
**Therefore with joy shall ye draw water out
of the wells of salvation. And in that day
shall ye say, Praise the Lord, call upon his
name, declare his doings among all people,
make mention that his name is exalted.**
Isaiah 12:3-4

When you are saved, you should joyfully testify of
your salvation and declare all of God's doings among all
people. Are you joyfully sharing your testimony of Jesus
with people?

Does God work through testimonies today?

YES! Let me share a testimony with you.

One day I met a man at my business. I had hired him
to haul some material away. We talked a little and I told
him I had a cassette tape called "The Healing Testimony"
and I wanted to give him a copy of it, but I had forgotten
to bring it and left it at home. I said, *"Since I forgot the
tape, could I just tell you about what is on it?"*
He said, *"OK."*
I told him how I had been saved. How Jesus changed

my life. How Jesus healed me of what the doctors called an incurable blood disease. After I shared that with him, he asked if I would still give him a copy of the tape. I said, *"Yes"* and he followed me home.

I gave him the tape and he said, *"I must go now."*

When he said that, I put my hand on his shoulder and asked, *"Can I pray for you?"*

He replied, *"Yes."*

I prayed for him and he cried. I asked him if he was ready to receive Jesus.

He said, *"I CAN'T do it!"*

The Holy Spirit led me to look him straight in the eyes and to say, *"In the name of the Lord Jesus Christ, I command that his tongue be set free now in Jesus' Name."* Again I asked him, *"Are you ready to receive Jesus?"*

He said, *"YES I AM!"* He prayed and asked Jesus to come into his heart and change his life. This all happened on a Friday.

On Monday the man's wife called and she said, *"I don't know what you did to my husband, but this is the first weekend in thirteen years that my husband has not been drunk."* Praise God! He is still saving and setting the captive free!

YES! God works through testimonies today! Will you allow God to use your testimony?

GOD'S WILL:
And I, if I be lifted up from the earth, will draw all men unto me.
John 12:32

Jesus knew that he would be lifted up on the cross. The IF was not for then; it was for the future. The IF was for you and me. The IF was for all Christians. 'And I, if I be lifted up.' I believe Jesus was saying that if those who believe in Him will continue to lift up His Name, continue to share testimony to His glory, then He will draw all men unto Himself. The man I just told you about was saved because Jesus was lifted up in the sharing of a testimony.

GOD'S WILL:
And I, if I be lifted up from the earth, will draw all men unto me.
John 12:32

The word draw in the Greek means to drag. When Jesus was lifted up and that man made the choice to receive Jesus, Jesus dragged him out of the hand of the enemy. He saved his soul, broke a thirteen-year alcohol addiction, and restored a husband to his wife and a father to his children.

Yes! God anoints & uses testimonies.

Will you allow Jesus to use YOUR testimony?

The complete teaching on
"How God can use Your Testimony" is available in the "Equipping the Saints" series, tape no. 2. See Item No. 2 on order form in back of book.

CHAPTER 10
Can I Hear
God's Voice?

Do you hear from God?

GOD'S WILL:
**My sheep hear my voice, and I know them,
and they follow me.**

John 10:27

"My sheep hear my voice." That's a promise of God's Word.

YES! You can hear from God!

GOD'S WILL:
**My sheep hear my voice, and I know them,
and they follow me.**

John 10:27

"His sheep hear His voice." "And they follow Him."

His sheep, God's people, are to hear His voice, *(His directions, His commands),* and follow Him *(be obedient to hear and to do what God has spoken to them).*

HEAR and OBEY

GOD'S WILL:
**When Jesus came into the coasts of
Caesarea Philippi, he asked his disciples,
saying, Whom do men say that I the Son
of man am? And they said, Some say that
thou art John the Baptist: some, Elias; and**

others, Jeremias, or one of the prophets.
He saith unto them, But whom say ye that
I am? And Simon Peter answered and said,
"Thou art the Christ, the Son the living
God. And Jesus answered and said unto
him, Blessed art thou, Simon Barjona: for
flesh and blood hath not revealed it unto
thee, but my Father which is in heaven.
Matthew 16:13-17

These verses contain three very important Truths! These are all part of the rock that the church is to be built on.

    1. Jesus is the Anointed One.

    2. Jesus is the Son of the Living God.

    3. Simon Peter heard from God.

The church is to be built on all three of these truths. Lets look a little closer at the third one — Simon Peter heard from God.

GOD'S WILL:
And Jesus answered and said unto him,
Blessed art thou, Simon Barjona: for flesh
and blood hath not revealed it unto thee,
but my Father which is in heaven.
Matthew 16:17

Jesus said, *'Simon Peter, you are blessed, because no man has told you who I am, but you have heard it from my Father in heaven.'*

GOD'S WILL:
And I say also unto thee, That thou art Pe-
ter, and upon this rock I will build my
church; and the gates of hell shall not pre-
vail against it.
Matthew 16:18

Upon what Rock?

Upon the rock *(the Revelation)* that Simon Peter heard directly from the Father. Upon the Revelation that you and I can hear from the Father just as Simon Peter did.

YES! You and I can hear from God today.

GOD'S WILL:
> **And I say also unto thee, That thou art Peter, and upon this rock I will build my church; and the gates of hell shall not prevail against it.**
> **Matthew 16:18**

And the gates of hell shall not prevail against it.

Against what?

Against the *revelation* that we can *hear* from the Father today. Against the voice of God when we hear and obey. That same voice that speaks to us and directs our steps is the same voice that spoke the world into existence. The gates of hell are no match for God. The gates of hell are no match for you when you are being directed by the voice of God.

GOD'S WILL:
> **And I say also unto thee, That thou art Peter, and upon this rock I will build my church; and the gates of hell shall not prevail against it.**
> **Matthew 16:18**

Who will build the church?

"And upon this rock I will build my church." Jesus said He will build the church.

How will Jesus build the church?

And upon this rock I will build my church. Jesus said he would build the church upon this rock. Jesus was saying that He would build the church on the *revelation* that Simon Peter heard from the Father. So it is what the Father is saying that the church is to be built on, and it is what the Father is saying — that the gates of hell can not prevail against.

GOD'S WILL:
For my thoughts are not your thoughts, neither are your ways my ways, saith the LORD. For as the heavens are higher than the earth, so are my ways higher than your ways, and my thoughts than your thoughts. For as the rain cometh down, and the snow from heaven, and returneth not thither, but watereth the earth, and maketh it bring forth and bud, that it may give seed to the sower, and bread to the eater: So shall my word be that goeth forth out of my mouth: it shall not return unto me void, but it shall accomplish that which I please, and it shall prosper in the thing whereto I sent it.

Isaiah 55:8-11

"So shall my Word be . . . "

Who's word? . . . Gods Word.

When God speaks, His Word will not come back void. When God speaks, His Word will hit the mark; it will accomplish; it will prosper. It will do what it was sent out to do. The gates of hell will not prevail against God's Word. When God speaks to you that which He has told you to do is already done. All you have to do is be obedient.

GOD'S WILL:
> **Then answered Jesus and said unto them, Verily, verily, I say unto you, The Son can do nothing of himself, but what he seeth the Father do: for what things so ever he doeth, these also doeth the Son likewise.**
> **John 5:19**

Jesus is our example. He only did what the Father was doing. Jesus always prospered because everything He did was based on hearing from the Father.

GOD'S WILL:
> **And he said, Abba, Father, all things are possible unto thee; take away this cup from me: nevertheless not what I will, but what thou wilt.**
> **Mark 14:36**

"Not what I will, But what thou will." Jesus always did the Fathers will!

How do we hear from the Father?

How do we find out God's will for our lives?

When Jesus went to be with the Father, did He make a provision for us to hear from God?

GOD'S WILL:
> **But the Comforter, which is the Holy Ghost, whom the Father will send in my name, he shall teach you all things, and bring all things to your remembrance, whatsoever I have said unto you.**
> **John 14:26**

GOD'S WILL:

But when the Comforter is come, whom I will send unto you from the Father, even the spirit of truth, which proceedeth from the Father, he shall testify of me.

John 15:26

The Holy Spirit proceedeth from the Father.

GOD'S WILL:

Howbeit when he, the Spirit of truth, is come, he will guide you into all truth: for he shall not speak of himself; but whatsoever he shall hear, that shall he speak; and he will shew you things to come. For He shall not speak of Himself; but whatsoever he shall hear.

John 16:13

GOD'S WILL:

He shall glorify me: for he shall receive of mine, and shall shew it unto you. All things that the Father hath are mine: therefore said I, that he shall take of mine, and shall shew it unto you.

John 16:14-15

All things of the Father belong to Jesus. The Holy Spirit will show us the things of Jesus. When the Holy Spirit shows us the things of Jesus, we are seeing the things of the Father. When the Holy Spirit speaks to us the things that He has heard, we are hearing from the Father. When we are obedient to what the Holy Spirit speaks, we are doing what the Father is doing and the gates of hell shall not prevail against us.

How does God speak to us today through the Holy Spirit?

Some of the ways are:

1. Word of God, the Bible
2. Audible Voice
3. Still, Small Voice
4. Visions
5. Dreams
6. Through other Believers
7. Inner Witness

TESTIMONY

After I had been a Christian for about one and a half years, I was invited to share my testimony at a church in Arkansas. When it was time to speak, I kept thinking of a certain scripture over and over again. I asked, *"God, do you want me to read that scripture?"* That still, small voice said, *"Yes."*

So there I was, in a church a thousand miles from home. I was asked to come to share my testimony and God was taking me in a completely different and new direction. Prior to this, I had shared my testimony a few times but never really preached the Word or ministered to people.

What would you do in this situation? Would you follow man's program? Would you follow the Holy Spirit? If this was in YOUR church, would there be enough liberty to allow the speaker *to follow the Holy Spirit?*

Being young in the Lord and wanting so much to please God, I went up to the pulpit and shared the scripture He gave me:

GOD'S WILL:
   And it shall come to pass afterward, that I will pour out my spirit upon all flesh; and your sons and your daughters shall prophesy, your old men shall dream dreams, your young men shall see visions.
                                    Joel 2:28

As soon as I read that scripture, the Holy Spirit brought to my mind what to do next. I said, *"I believe it is God's desire for all the children to come up and to be prayed for."* As I spoke, every child immediately came forward.

As I prayed for the first little boy, the power of God came over him and he fell under the power. The next thing I knew, their were a dozen children between eight and fifteen lying on the floor under the hand of God. My plan was to share my testimony. Man's plan was for me to share my testimony. God's plan was to minister to these young people.

Those young folks laid under the power of God for over an hour. During this time, we worshipped the Lord. Then He gave me another scripture. So I went up and read it.

GOD'S WILL:

But he was wounded for our transgressions, he was bruised for our iniquities: the chastisement of our peace was upon him; and with his stripes we are healed.
Isaiah 53:5

Again, as soon as I read it, the Holy Spirit told me what to do next. I was to tell those that needed an emotional or physical healing in their body to raise their hand. Then I was to have those who believed that God would meet the needs of those with their hands raised, to go to them and pray.

At this time, all of the children that had been under the power of God went to their parents, the adults, and prayed for them. The power of God touched the adults and they fell under the power. It was so wonderful to see those young folks praying for the adults.

GOD'S WILL:
But he answered and said, It is written, Man shall not live by bread alone, but by every word that proceedeth out of the mouth of God.

Matthew 4:4

We need the proceeding Word. We need that Word that God speaks for a specific time and place.

When the proceeding Word comes forth from God through the Holy Spirit and we are obedient to the Word, the power of God is released, and that Word will accomplish what it was sent to do.

The proceeding Word of God that night was the two scriptures He gave us, and the direction to pray for the children and those that needed healing. All were blessed because the proceeding Word from God was obeyed.

The gates of hell could not prevail against the Word that God had spoken for that place and for that time. That night, I heard from the Father just like Simon Peter heard from the Father. And this day you, too can hear from the Father.

Press in; seek God; meditate on the Word; sit at Jesus's feet; find out what the Father is saying; OBEY Him, and everything you do will hit the mark. Neither the devil nor the gates of hell can stop what God has told you to do. God's Word always prospers where He sends it.

A teaching on
"Hearing God's Voice" is available
in the "Equipping the Saints" series, tape no. 3.
See Item No. 2 on order form in back of book.

CHAPTER 11
But One Thing
Is Needful!

What is the one thing that Jesus said is needful?

GOD'S WILL:
> **Now it came to pass, as they went, that he entered into a certain village; and a certain woman named Martha received him into her house.**
>
> **Luke 10:38**

Martha received Jesus and His disciples into her home.

GOD'S WILL:
> **And she had a sister called Mary, which also sat at Jesus' feet, and heard his word.**
>
> **Luke 10:39**

Mary chose Jesus. Mary chose to hear the word from Jesus.

GOD'S WILL:
> **But Martha was cumbered about much serving, and came to him, and said, Lord, dost thou not care that my sister hath left me to serve alone? bid her therefore that she help me.**
>
> **Luke 10:40**

Martha was carrying a heavy load. She was burdened and trying to provide for Jesus and the disciples physical needs *(food, shelter)*. Martha was upset that Mary would not help her meet the natural needs of Jesus and the disciples. Martha was saying, *"Jesus, I'm doing everything. Would you tell my sister what is important here? Would you tell her to get up and help me?"*

GOD'S WILL:
And Jesus answered and said unto her, Martha, Martha, thou art careful and troubled about many things:
Luke 10:41

Jesus said, *"Dear Martha, you are anxious and worried about so many things."*

GOD'S WILL:
But one thing is needful: and Mary hath chosen that good part, which shall not be taken away from her.
Luke 10:42

Jesus told Martha that only one thing was necessary, and Mary chose it by sitting at His feet. Mary chose the good part and it would never be taken away from her. Jesus was saying, *"Yes, my disciples and I need some things in the natural. We need food; we need a place to stay; but Martha, more important than these things, is your time spent with me. Your time spent sitting at my feet. Your time spent listening to my Word."*

GOD'S WILL:
But one thing is needful: and Mary hath chosen that good part, which shall not be taken away from her.
Luke 10:42

"Which shall not be taken away from her." There is something that happens at Jesus' feet that no trial, no tribulation, no demon can steal from you. Jesus said what Mary received at His feet was the good part and it would not be taken away from her.

GOD'S WILL:
In the beginning was the Word, and the Word was with God, and the Word was God. The same was in the beginning with God. All things were made by him; and without him was not any thing made that was made. In him was life; and the life was the light of men.
John 1:1-4

GOD'S WILL:
And the word was made flesh, and dwelt among us, (and we beheld his glory, the glory as of the only begotten of the Father,) full of grace and truth.
John 1:14

The Word was made flesh. Jesus was made flesh. Jesus is *the* Word. The Word is Jesus.

GOD'S WILL:
And she had a sister called Mary, which also sat at Jesus' feet, and heard his word.
Luke 10:39

Mary chose Jesus. Jesus was *the* Word. Mary chose *the* Word.

GOD'S WILL:
But one thing is needful: and Mary hath chosen that good part, which shall not be taken away from her.

Luke 10:42

Jesus said, *"But one thing is needful,"* (but one thing is important). Jesus said Mary chose that good part and it will not be taken away from her.

What did Mary choose? JESUS. Who was Jesus in the beginning? The WORD. Mary chose "THE WORD."

Have you chosen the good part?
Have you chosen the Word?

But one thing is needful.

GOD'S WILL:
And take the helmet of salvation, and the sword of the Spirit, which is the word of God.

Ephesians 6:17

The sword of the Spirit is the Word of God. Let's look at how Jesus used the sword of the Spirit.

GOD'S WILL:
Then was Jesus led up of the Spirit into the wilderness to be tempted of the devil. And when he had fasted forty days and forty nights, he was afterward an hungered. And when the tempter came to him, he said, If thou be the Son of God, command that these stones be made bread. But he answered and said, It is written, Man shall not live by bread alone, but by every word that proceedeth out of the mouth of God.

Matthew 4:1-4

When Jesus was tempted by the devil, He answered with His spiritual sword. He answered with the Word of God. Jesus said, *"It is written."* This is what the Word says.

GOD'S WILL:

Then the devil taketh Him up into the holy city, and setteth Him on a pinnacle of the temple, And saith unto Him, If thou be the Son of God, cast thyself down: for it is written, He shall give his angels charge concerning thee: and in their hands they shall bear thee up, lest at any time thou dash thy foot against a stone. Jesus said unto him, It is written again, Thou shalt not tempt the Lord thy God.

Matthew 4:5-7

Again, Jesus answered with the Word. "IT IS WRITTEN." He took all that the devil tried to throw at Him and cut it to pieces with the sword of the Spirit, the Word of God.

GOD'S WILL:

Again, the devil taketh him up into an exceeding high mountain, and sheweth him all the kingdoms of the world, and the glory of them; And saith unto him, All these things will I give thee, if thou wilt fall down and worship me. Then saith Jesus unto him, Get thee hence, Satan: for it is written, Thou shalt worship the Lord thy God, and him only shalt thou serve.

Matthew 4:8-10

Again, Jesus is tempted. Again Jesus says, "IT IS WRITTEN." Just fight the temptations of the enemy with the Word of God! Remember, Jesus said, "But one thing is needful."

THE WORD. THE BIBLE.

GOD'S WILL:
Then the devil leaveth him, and, behold, angels came and ministered unto Him.
Matthew 4:11

Jesus fought off satan's attacks with the sword of the Spirit, The Word of God. Jesus is our example. If we are going to stand against the devil, we must have the one thing that is needful:

THE WORD.

GOD'S WILL:
For the word of God is quick, and powerful, and sharper than any two-edged sword, piercing even to the dividing asunder of soul and spirit, and of the joints and marrow, and is a discerner of the thoughts and intents of the heart.
Hebrews 4:12

- THE WORD IS QUICK *(Alive, Living)*
- THE WORD IS POWERFUL *(Active, Working, Energizing, Never Dormant)*
- THE WORD IS SHARPER *(Penetrating, Convicting)* THAN ANY TWO-EDGED SWORD.
- THE WORD IS PIERCING *(It Goes Through)*
- THE WORD DIVIDES *(Separates)* BETWEEN WHAT IS SOUL *(Mind, Will, Emotions)* AND WHAT IS SPIRIT *(Of God)*

- THE WORD IS A DISCERNER *(Judges, Sifts and Analyzes)* OF THE THOUGHTS AND INTENTIONS OF THE HEART.

Remember Jesus said, *"But one thing is needful and that one thing would not be taken away from Mary."*

Mary chose "THE WORD."

Mary chose what is Alive, Active, Working, Energizing, Never Dormant, Piercing, Dividing, Separating. Mary chose "THE WORD."

When you choose the Word, it becomes part of you, it becomes who you are, it will lead you, it will guide you, it will separate between your mind, will and emotions and what God's Plan is for your life.

"But one thing is needful."

GOD'S WILL:
Thy Word is a lamp unto my feet, and a light unto my path.
Psalms 119:105

The Word will guide you.

"But one thing is needful."

GOD'S WILL:
Thy Word have I hid in mine heart, that I might not sin against thee.
Psalms 119:11

The Word will become part of you. It will keep you from sinning.

"But one thing is needful."

GOD'S WILL:
   So then faith cometh by hearing, and hearing by the word of God.

                                   Romans 10:17

The Word produces faith.

"But one thing is needful."

GOD'S WILL:
   Wherefore laying aside all malice, and all guile, and hypocrisies, and envies, and all evil speakings, As newborn babes, desire the sincere milk of the word, that ye may grow thereby:

                                   1 Peter 2:1-2

The Word makes you grow.

GOD'S WILL:
   Being born again, not of corruptible seed, but of incorruptible, by the word of God, which liveth and abideth for ever.

                                   1 Peter 1:23

The Word LASTS forever.

GOD'S WILL:
   Now when they saw the boldness of Peter and John, and perceived that they were unlearned and ignorant men, they marvelled; and they took knowledge of them, that they had been with Jesus.

                                   Acts 4:13

The boldness of Peter and John was a result of being with Jesus. *(The Word)* When you spend time in the Word, the world will see that same boldness in you.

"But one thing is needful."

GOD'S WILL:
   My son, attend to my words; incline thine ear unto my sayings.
                                    Proverbs 4:20

My son, PAY ATTENTION and obey my words; LISTEN to what I'm telling you.

GOD'S WILL:
   Let them not depart from thine eyes; keep them in the midst of thine heart.
                                    Proverbs 4:21

Keep my words before your eyes which will keep them in your heart.

GOD'S WILL:
   For they are life unto those that find them, and health to all their flesh.
                                    Proverbs 4:22

For my Word is life to those who will search them (read them) and my Word brings health (healing) to your body.

GOD'S WILL:
   Keep thy heart with all diligence; for out of it are the issues of life.
                                    Proverbs 4:23

Protect; be careful about what you put in your heart *(what comes before your eyes or what you read is what you will have in your heart)*. For what's in your heart will determine how you react to all the issues of life that you will face. If your heart is filled with the Word, you

will react as Jesus would. You will say, "It is written."
This is what the Word says. It doesn't matter what I see
or hear in the natural realm. I LIVE BY WHAT IS WRIT-
TEN.

"But one thing is needful."

GOD'S WILL:
**For they are life unto those that find them,
and health to all their flesh.**
Proverbs 4:22

When I received Jesus as my Savior, I had a blood
disease. Ten months after I received Jesus, I was totally
healed. During the first three months of knowing Jesus,
I read the complete Bible. It was the reading of God's
Word that set the stage for my healing; the Word brought
health to all my flesh.

"But one thing is needful."

GOD'S WILL:
**This book of the law shall not depart out
of thy mouth; but thou shalt meditate
therein day and night, that thou mayest
observe to do according to all that is written therein: for then thou shalt make thy
way prosperous, and then thou shalt have
good success.**
Joshua 1:8

Prosperity and Success come from the Word.

GOD'S WILL:
**Blessed is the man that walketh not in the
counsel of the ungodly, nor standeth in
the way of sinners, nor sitteth in the seat**

**of the scornful. But his delight is in the
law of the LORD; and in his law doth he
meditate day and night. And he shall be
like a tree planted by the rivers of water,
that bringeth forth his fruit in his season;
his leaf also shall not wither; and whatsoever he doeth shall prosper.**

Psalms 1:1-3

Meditating day and night in the Word brings forth fruit
and will make your way prosperous.

"But one thing is needful."

Do you think it would be wise to give most of your
time to the one thing Jesus said is needful, **"The Word?"**
How much time do you spend in the Word? How much
time do you spend on:

*Ball Games • Friends • Television • Hobbies
Church Events • Telephone Calls • Work
Sports • Ministry • Family • Shopping
Fellowship • Vacations*

Compare the time you spend on all these things to
the time you spend at Jesus' feet in His Word. Jesus
said,

"But one thing is needful."

THE WORD.

*A teaching on
"But One Thing Is Needful" is available
in the "Equipping the Saints" series, tape no. 4.
See Item No. 2 on order form in back of book.*

CHAPTER 12
Faith Cometh By Hearing, and Hearing By The Word of God
Part 1

GOD'S WILL:
So then faith cometh by hearing, and hearing by the word of God.
Romans 10:17

Could this be you or someone that you know?

I have been a Christian for over twenty years and I have never led a lost person to Jesus.

"Can I change?"
"YES!"
"Can God still use me after all these years?"
"YES!"
"Can I really be used of God to reach a lost person?"
"YES!"
"But how?"

BY FAITH! The same way you received Jesus as Savior. BY FAITH!

"But I just don't have faith in this area. I just don't believe God can use me to reach a lost person."

THAT'S OK! To solve a problem we must first admit to having one. Lack of faith is doubt and unbelief. Confess your doubt and unbelief as sin and ask God to forgive you and help you. Then take steps to build your faith.

"But how?"

The Bible says:

GOD'S WILL:
So then faith cometh by hearing, and hear-
ing by the word of God.

Romans 10:17

Faith comes by hearing, so let's start building faith by hearing the following testimony.

A beautiful young lady was born again at age thirteen. She married a non-Christian when she was seventeen. She prayed for the salvation of her husband for nineteen years. God was faithful and saved Him. She told her children about Jesus but never told anyone else about Him. In the church she was part of, she was never discipled or trained to be a witness for Jesus.

After her husband was saved, God worked through him to win souls for Jesus. As she watched and listened, she desired to be used by God to reach the lost. The more she saw and heard, the stronger the desire grew to be used by God to win a lost person.

REMEMBER! FAITH COMES BY HEARING. As her faith started to grow, she would let God reach out to people through her by offering to pray for them.

The first time this happened, she was having lunch with her husband. He looked at her and said, *"Whatever God has told you to do, just do it."* God was prompting her to go and pray for someone at the next table. After being encouraged, she went to the next table and prayed for that person. At this time, she had been a Christian for about twenty five years, and this was the first time she ever reached out to a person like that.

IT'S NEVER TOO LATE! During the next couple of years, she prayed for several people in restaurants as the

Lord would lead her and many times people would tell her the next time they saw her how God had healed them.

That gift was always in her. She just needed her faith built up to use it. As she allowed God to use her, her faith got stronger and stronger.

One day she stopped in a convenience store to buy a bottle of water. While in the store, she gave a cassette tape with a testimony on it to the cashier. This allowed her to start a conversation with the cashier. Through that conversation, the cashier asked Jesus to be her Savior. *That's something to shout about! Praise God!*

She was a Christian for twenty eight years before leading a lost soul to Jesus. It does not matter how long it has been. If you want to change, God will help you.

One month later, she received a phone call inquiring about some property she had listed in the newspaper. Before she hung up the phone, the lady on the other end had asked Jesus to be her Savior. *Again, that's something to shout about!*

In this testimony, we see two important things happen:

1. Two souls are saved.
2. A person's faith can be built up to believe that Jesus can use them to reach the lost.

God can and wants to use every person who knows Jesus Christ as their Savior. Everyone is included. There is no such thing as those who are too old or even, too young.

I believe your faith is already starting to rise up. I can hear you saying, *"I can do this. I can do this. I can. I can. I can. I will!"*

GOD'S WILL:
So then faith cometh by hearing, and hearing by the word of God.
                    Romans 10:17

OK. Let's build your faith some more. Let's see what the Word says.

GOD'S WILL:
I can do all things through Christ which strengtheneth me.
Philippians 4:13

ALL THINGS. That includes winning the lost.

Say: *"I can win souls through Christ which strengthens me."* Say it again. *"I can win souls through Christ which strengthens me."*
Confess this daily! Every day! Make it a habit. It's not what you do occasionally that will make you effective. It's what you do habitually that will make you effective.

GOD'S WILL:
If God be for us, who can be against us?
Romans 8:31B

Say: *"If God be for me, nobody can stop me from winning souls for Jesus!"*

GOD'S WILL:
For with God nothing shall be impossible.
Luke 1:37

Say: *"Nothing is impossible with God, and that includes God using me to reach the lost. I **can** be used of God to reach a lost and dying world."*

GOD'S WILL:
Verily, verily, I say unto you, He that believeth on me, the works that I do shall

he do also; and greater works than these shall he do; because I go unto my Father.
John 14:12

Say: *"Jesus said I would do **greater works** and that includes using me to win the lost."*

GOD'S WILL:
For God hath not given us the spirit of fear; but of power, and of love, and of a sound mind.
2 Timothy 1:7

GOD'S WILL:
. . . for God is love.
1 John 4:8B

GOD'S WILL:
There is no fear in love; but perfect love casteth out fear: because fear hath torment. He that feareth is not made perfect in love.
1 John 4:18

Say: *"God is love; God is in me; there is no fear in God, and there is no fear in me. Fear cannot stop me from winning the lost for Jesus."*

GOD'S WILL:
Nay, in all these things we are more than conquerors through him that loved us.
Romans 8:37

Say: *"I am more than a conqueror through Christ. I am more than able to conquer fears, pride, and anything else that would try to stop me from being a witness for Jesus. Through Him (Jesus) that loves me, I can win the lost."*

Can you feel your faith level rising?

You keep building up your faith to win the lost, and one day that DAM WILL BURST. All that word, all those faith-filled scriptures will go forth, and they will not return void.

GOD'S WILL:
So shall my word be that goeth forth out of my mouth: it shall not return unto me void, but it shall accomplish that which I please, and it shall prosper in the thing whereto I sent it.

Isaiah 55:11

Say: *"I will speak God's word to the lost; it will go forth and it will not return void; it shall accomplish what God pleases; it shall prosper, it shall be fruitful, and souls will be saved."*

GOD'S WILL:
I am the vine, ye are the branches: He that abideth in me, and I in him, the same bringeth forth much fruit: for without me ye can do nothing.

John 15:5

Say: *"I am a branch, I abide in Jesus, and He abideth in me. I can do nothing by myself; but through Jesus, that is in me, I will bring forth much fruit. I will win the lost."*

GOD'S WILL:
If ye abide in me, and my words abide in you, ye shall ask what ye will, and it shall be done unto you.

John 15:7

Say: *"I abide in Jesus and His words abide in me. I am asking for souls to be saved and **they** shall be."*

Faith cometh by hearing, and hearing by the Word of God.

GOD'S WILL:

This book of the law shall not depart out of thy mouth; but thou shalt meditate therein day and night, that thou mayest observe to do according to all that is written therein: for then thou shalt make thy way prosperous, and then thou shalt have good success.

Joshua 1:8

OK. It's your turn. Get out your Bible. Search the scriptures and apply them to your life and winning the lost. Write them out just as we have here and confess them daily. Write out and send to us all the verses God shows you which apply to building your faith to win the lost.

Every morning, pray for divine appointments. Pray, *"God, use me today. God, bring someone into my path today that I can share Jesus with."*

Say: *"I will meditate on the word; my way shall be prosperous and I shall have good success at winning the lost."*

Faith works!

Will you apply your faith to your life and winning the lost? Will you meditate on the Word and apply your faith in the area of winning souls as hard as you would apply it for:

A New Car?

Your Ministry?

A New House?

Your Job?

A Dream Vacation?

A Spouse?

Prosperity?

A New Church Building?

A Healing?

Your Children?

A New Sound System?

New Carpet for the Church?

Stuff?

Would you apply your faith as diligently to win souls as you would for the things listed above?

Would you?

Meditate on the Word of God and let the Word increase your faith for reaching the Lost!
Then apply your faith and go tell somebody about Jesus!

CHAPTER 13
Faith Cometh By Hearing, and Hearing By The Word of God
Part 2

GOD'S WILL:
So then faith cometh by hearing, and hearing by the word of God.

Romans 10:17

In Part 1, we talked about a person that had been a Christian over twenty years and had never led a lost person to Jesus. Chances are, that person said something like this:

"I'm just not capable enough in leading someone to Jesus. I'm just not smart enough to lead someone to Jesus. I'm just not educated enough to lead someone to Jesus. I'm too shy to tell someone about Jesus. I'm afraid to tell someone about Jesus."

That is a *negative* confession.

GOD'S WILL:
For verily I say unto you, That whosoever shall say unto this mountain, Be thou removed, and be thou cast into the sea; and shall not doubt in his heart, but shall believe that those things which he saith shall come to pass; he shall have whatsoever he saith.

Mark 11:23

The Bible says we can have what we say when we Believe in our hearts and CONFESS with our mouth. If you have made negative confessions like those just listed, then you will have the negative things you have confessed. If you say, "I can't win lost souls, I'm not capable enough, I'm not smart enough," then you will never be able to. First you must change **YOUR CONFESSION,** which will help change your belief, which will help change your actions.

GOD'S WILL:
So then faith cometh by hearing, and hearing by the word of God.
Romans 10:17

Confess: *"I can win the lost; I am capable of winning the lost; I am smart enough for Jesus to use me."* Confess the Positive! Confess the Truth! Confess the Word of God!"

As you confess the truth regularly, daily, faith will build up in your heart, then you will have what you believe in your heart and confess with your mouth.

Confess: *"I am a soul winner."*

Say It.

I am a soul winner. Go ahead — say it. *"I am a soul winner."* Now believe it.

GOD'S WILL:
For in him dwelleth all the fulness of the Godhead bodily. And ye are complete in him, which is the head of all principality and power:
Colossians 2:9-10

The *"In Him"* means "In Christ." You are complete in Christ.

Confess: *"I am complete in Christ. I am so complete that I am fully equipped to win the lost for Jesus."*

Say it again. Believe it in your heart. Keep saying it until you believe it.

GOD'S WILL:

Then he called his twelve disciples together, and gave them power and authority over all devils, and to cure diseases.

Luke 9:1

Confess: *"I have power & authority over all devils and diseases. I can take authority over devils and diseases before the unsaved, and through this, many will get saved."*

GOD'S WILL:

Behold, I give unto you power to tread on serpents and scorpions, and over all the power of the enemy: and nothing shall by any means hurt you.

Luke 10:19

Confess: *"I have been given power to tread on all devils and demons. I have power over all their abilities, and nothing they do can hurt me. Nothing they do can stop me from being a powerful witness for Jesus."*

GOD'S WILL:

Which he wrought in Christ, when he raised him from the dead, and set him at his own right hand in the heavenly places, Far above all principality, and power, and might, and dominion, and every name that is named, not only in this world, but also in that which is to come: And hath put all things under his feet, and gave him to be the head over all things to the church, Which is his body, the fullness of him that filleth all in all.

Ephesians 1:20-23

GOD'S WILL:
And hath raised us up together, and made us sit together in heavenly places in Christ Jesus:

Ephesians 2:6

Confess: *"I sit in heavenly places with Jesus. I am far above devils and demonic forces, and they are under my feet, and what is under my feet in no way can stop me from leading the lost to Jesus."*

GOD'S WILL:
But ye shall receive power, after that the Holy Ghost is come upon you: and ye shall be witnesses unto me both in Jerusalem, and in all Judæa, and in Samaria, and unto the uttermost part of the earth.

Acts 1:8

Confess: *"I have received power; the Holy Ghost has come upon me. I am a witness in my neighborhood, in my city, in the close places and the far-away places. I am a powerful witness."*

GOD'S WILL:
I can do all things through Christ which strengtheneth me.

Philippians 4:13

Confess: *"I can win the lost through Christ who strengthens me."* Say it again. Say it again. Keep saying it until you believe it in your heart. *"I can win the lost through Christ who strengthens me."*

GOD'S WILL:
And he said unto them, Go ye into all the world, and preach the gospel to every creature. He that believeth and is baptized shall be saved; but he that believeth not shall be damned.

Mark 16:15-16

Confess: *"I do confess the gospel, that Jesus died to reconcile lost souls to the Father, to every person I meet; they do believe, and they are saved and baptized."*

GOD'S WILL:
And Jesus came and spake unto them, saying, All power is given unto me in heaven and in earth. Go ye therefore, and teach all nations, baptizing them in the name of the Father, and of the Son, and of the Holy Ghost: Teaching them to observe all things whatsoever I have commanded you; and, lo, I am with you alway, even unto the end of the world. Amen.

Matthew 28:18-20

Confess: *"As I go, each day, wherever I am, I tell people about Jesus. I do not go alone. Jesus, and the authority He has delegated to me, go with me."*

> *Can you feel it?*
> *Feel what?*
> *Faith!*
> *As you confess the Word.*
> *As you confess the truth.*

As you confess the positive, you are hearing, faith-filled words come out of your mouth. They are being sown into your heart, and you will have a fruitful harvest.

GOD'S WILL:

And he shall be like a tree planted by the rivers of water, that bringeth forth his fruit in his season; his leaf also shall not wither; and whatsoever he doeth shall prosper.

Psalms 1:3

Confess: *"Whatsoever I do shall prosper! When I tell people about Jesus, I will be successful!"*

GOD'S WILL:

Delight thyself also in the Lord; and he shall give thee the desires of thine heart. Commit thy way unto the Lord; trust also in him; and he shall bring it to pass.

Psalms 37:4-5

Confess: *"The desire of my heart is to win souls for Jesus. I am committing my way to Him. I am trusting in Him and He will bring it to pass."*

GOD'S WILL:

For ever, O Lord, thy word is settled in heaven.

Psalms 119:89

Confess: *"The Word says I am a witness for Jesus and that settles it! The end. Nobody or nothing can stop me."*

GOD'S WILL:

Ye are of God, little children, and have overcome them: because greater is he that is in you, than he that is in the world.

1 John 4:4

Confess: *"The Holy Spirit lives in me. He is Jesus' witness, He is greater than any obstacle that I can run up against while telling people about Jesus."*

GOD'S WILL:
Therefore if any man be in Christ, he is a new creature: old things are passed away; behold, all things are become new. And all things are of God, who hath reconciled us to himself by Jesus Christ, and hath given to us the ministry of reconciliation;
2 Corinthians 5:17-18

Confess: *"I am a new creature. I am of God. I have been reconciled to God by Jesus. He has given me the ministry of reconciliation. I am a minister of reconciliation. I am helping sinful men to find their way to God by telling them what Jesus Christ has done for them."*

GOD'S WILL:
Now then we are ambassadors for Christ, as though God did beseech you by us: we pray you in Christ's stead, be ye reconciled to God.
2 Corinthians 5:20

Confess: *"I am an ambassador (a representative) for Jesus. I am begging people to accept what God has done for them."*

GOD'S WILL:
And that he died for all, that they which live should not henceforth live unto themselves, but unto him which died for them, and rose again.
2 Corinthians 5:15

Confess: *"I am no longer living for myself. I am living for Christ who died for me. I am living for Christ by being His witness, all day, every day.*

GOD'S WILL:
And be not conformed to this world: but be ye transformed by the renewing of your mind, that ye may prove what is that good, and acceptable, and perfect, will of God.
Romans 12:2

Confess: *"By confessing the faith-filled truth of God's Word, I am renewing my mind. I am becoming a stronger witness for Jesus every time I confess it. I have a renewed mind, a positive confession, and I'm winning souls for Jesus daily."*

It is through the renewing of your mind by the Word of God, that you will become a DYNAMIC SOUL WINNER!

CHAPTER 14
The Shofar —
The Trumpet

God — Why are people being healed
when the Shofar is sounded?

"God, why does the atmosphere, or chemistry of a room change when the Shofar is sounded?" These were my questions.

I purchased a Shofar in Israel in May, 1996. In October of 1996, I felt led of the Lord to take it to Africa with us. Just before leaving for Africa, Carla had a dream. In that dream, she was pregnant. We were in a small car and I was taking her to the hospital. On the way to the hospital, I reached under the seat and pulled out this giant Shofar. I then said to her, *"I will blow the Shofar during the birthing process."* In obedience to God, we took and blew the Shofar. The following is part of a letter received after our trip to Africa:

October 1996, Kenya, Africa

Sister Phanice: *"The blowing of the trumpet (Shofar) you brought here didn't just make a noise. It declared 'Victory!' Demons were cast out! Captives were set free! It revealed that God is reigning in our city in a mighty way. Since you left, we have been having wonderful testimonies about healing, deliverance, and people being set free from evil powers and the Holy Spirit is leading people from one point of glory to another."*

Since then, I have blown the Shofar as the Lord leads and, wow, what God does when the trumpet is sounded!"

February 1997, Cold Water, Michigan

"Woman Set Free." She said, *"I have been bound by fear for over fifteen years. When the Shofar was sounded that fear left me. I have been set free. I feel so good, I'm free!"*

March 1998

A man needed rotator cuff surgery for his shoulder. He said, *"When the trumpet was sounded, something hit my shoulder. Pain left."* He never had to have surgery.

May 1998, Cleveland, Ohio

A man healed said: *"I have been in pain for over twenty days. I was hurting so much, that I wasn't going to come to church tonight. I only speak Spanish; and when the man (Jim Barbarossa) was speaking I could not understand him. But God spoke to me and said, 'When he blows that horn, something great is going to happen.' As soon as he blew the horn, the pain left my body. I am healed. You see, I can move my arm and shoulder without any pain. God has healed me!"*

September 1998, F.G.B.M.F.I. Dinner Meeting Holland, Michigan

A man healed said: *"I have been having trouble with my legs. When you blew that horn, God healed me!"*

September 1998, F.G.B.M.F.I. Holland, Michigan

Brother Ray: *"I have had pain in my right shoulder for a long time. I could not lift my arm above my shoulder. When you blew the Shofar, the pain left! I can lift my arm without pain. I am healed."*

October 1998, Woman Healed of Back Problem
Tulsa, Oklahoma
She had been in pain for four years! When the trumpet was sounded, pain left.

January 1999, Man Healed
"I have had a problem with my tailbone for a long time. I could never sit through one meeting without being in pain. When you blew that Shofar, the pain left my body and I have sat through 4 meetings without pain."

January 1999, Boy Healed
"I had a lump on my chest and was in pain. When the trumpet was sounded, the pain and the lump left."

February 1999, Christian Busisness Men's
Fellowship International; Hinsdale, Illinois
A man had been in pain for many years. Several times during the meeting, I saw him touch the left side of his face. As I blew the Shofar, I saw him grab his face. He came up at the end of the service. He said, *"I had shingles and was in severe pain but when the Shofar was sounded, the pain left. The pain was gone."* **Thank you Jesus!**

March 1999, Alabama
A lady had a blood clot in her leg. After the trumpet was sounded, the blood clot was gone.

August 1999, Connecticut
A lady had pain in her knees. When trumpet sounded, pain left.

September 1999, New York
A man had pain from a pinched sciatic nerve for two years. When the trumpet was sounded, pain left.

October 1999, Ohio

A young man had severe pain in his knees. When the trumpet was sounded, he jumped up and down without pain.

At this point, I had no biblical understanding of the Shofar or what was happening. All I know is when I saw that Shofar, I had to buy it, and that I needed to be obedient and blow it as God leads me. Since then, I have sought God for answers and searched the Bible, and I will do my best to share these things with you.

A Shofar is a horn from an animal, prepared to be used as a musical instrument. Shofars are usually made from the horn of a ram, wild goat, gazelle, antelope or kudu. The horn of a cow is never used because of the golden calf. *(Exodus, Chapter 32)*

Shofar is mentioned about seventy times in the Bible. You will find it as a trumpet or cornet.

There are two types of Shofars:

1. Ram's Horn Shofar

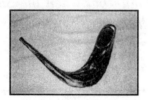

2. Yemenite Shofar
(larger of the two, usually 3' to 4' long.)

The Ram's Horn sounds like an animal crying. It is a repentant-type sound. The Yemenite sounds more like a modern trumpet. It has a jubilee sound, a celebration sound.

Who blows Shofars?

GOD'S WILL:

And he shall send his angels with a great sound of a trumpet, and they shall gather together his elect from the four winds, from one end of heaven to the other.

Matthew 24:31

Angels blow the Shofar.

GOD'S WILL:

For the Lord himself shall descend from heaven with a shout, with the voice of the archangel, and with the trump of God: and the dead in Christ shall rise first:

1 Thessalonians 4:16

Jesus blows the Shofar.

GOD'S WILL:

And it came to pass on the third day in the morning, that there were thunders and lightnings, and a thick cloud upon the mount, and the voice of the trumpet exceeding loud; so that all the people that was in the camp trembled. And Moses brought forth the people out of the camp to meet with God; and they stood at the nether part of the mount. And mount Sinai was altogether on a smoke, because the Lord descended upon it in fire: and the smoke thereof ascended as the smoke of a furnace, and the whole mount quaked greatly. And when the voice of the trumpet sounded long, and waxed louder and louder, Moses spake, and God answered him by a voice.

Exodus 19:16-19

God blows the Shofar.

GOD'S WILL:
And the sons of Aaron, the priests, shall blow with the trumpets; and they shall be to you for an ordinance for ever throughout your generations.

Numbers 10:8

The Priest blows the Shofar.

GOD'S WILL:
But ye are a chosen generation, a royal priesthood, a holy nation, a peculiar people; that ye should shew forth the praises of him who hath called you out of darkness into his marvellous light:

1 Peter 2:9

All Christians are Priests.

A Christian can blow the Shofar.

So, God blows the Shofar. Jesus blows the Shofar. Angels blow the Shofar. Man blows the Shofar. It must drive the devil crazy when he hears the Shofar. He does not know who is blowing it. Is it man, is it an angel, is it Jesus, is it the final great blast, is Jesus returning? Let's blow the Shofar and drive the enemy crazy!

Why is the sound of the Shofar so special?

GOD'S WILL:
I was in the spirit on the Lord's day, and heard behind me a great voice, as of a trumpet,

Revelation 1:10

GOD'S WILL:

After this I looked, and, behold, a door was opened in heaven: and the first voice which I heard was as it were of a trumpet talking with me; which said, Come up hither, and I will shew thee things which must be hereafter.

Revelation 4:1

The voice of God is like the sound of a trumpet.

Who does the air belong to?

GOD'S WILL:

Wherein in time past ye walked according to the course of this world, according to the prince of the power of the air, the spirit that now worketh in the children of disobedience:

Ephesians 2:2

The devil is the prince and power of the air. OK! Now what happens when you blow a Shofar? You release into the air *(the devil's camp)* the sound of the trumpet, which is like the voice of God. Each time you sound it, you are hammering the enemy's camp with the voice of God. That is why the atmosphere of a room changes when the trumpet is sounded. You are clearing the air between you and heaven. You drive back the enemy with each blast of the trumpet.

GOD'S WILL:

In the beginning God created the heaven and the earth. And the earth was without form, and void; and darkness was upon the face of the deep. And the spirit of God moved upon the face of the waters. And God said, Let there be light: and there was light.

Genesis 1:1-3

God said, God spoke, God created with his voice. When you blow a Shofar, you are releasing that which is like the voice of God. You are releasing God's power and anointing into the atmosphere.

Why are people healed when the trumpet is sounded?

GOD'S WILL:
And if ye go to war in your land against the enemy that oppresseth you, then ye shall blow an alarm with the trumpets; and ye shall be remembered before the Lord your God, and ye shall be saved from your enemies.

Numbers 10:9

Sickness is of the enemy that oppresseth you. When we blow the Shofar in obedience to the ordinance, God delivers people from the enemies that oppress them *(pain, sickness)*.

What effect does the blowing of the Shofar have on the enemy?

GOD'S WILL:
And they stood every man in his place round about the camp: and all the host ran, and cried, and fled. And the three hundred blew the trumpets, and the Lord set every man's sword against his fellow, even throughout all the host: and the host fled to Beth-shittah in Zererath, and to the border of Abelmeholah, unto Tabbath.

Judges 7:21-22

The enemy's camp went into confusion, and they turned on each other with the sword. Blow the Shofar in your city and send the enemy running.

What brought down the walls of Jericho?

GOD'S WILL:
So the people shouted when the priests blew with the trumpets: and it came to pass, when the people heard the sound of the trumpet, and the people shouted with a great shout, that the wall fell down flat, so that the people went up into the city, every man straight before him, and they took the city.
Joshua 6:20

The sound of the trumpet and a mighty shout brought down the walls. OBEDIENCE. Doing exactly what God said to do. At the very time He said to do it.

The Shofar is sometimes a call for Repentance.

GOD'S WILL:
Blow ye the trumpet in Zion, and sound an alarm in my holy mountain: let all the inhabitants of the land tremble: for the day of the Lord cometh, for it is nigh at hand;
Joel 2:1

GOD'S WILL:
Therefore also now, saith the Lord, turn ye even to me with all your heart, and with fasting, and with weeping, and with mourning: And rend your heart, and not your garments, and turn unto the Lord your God:

for he is gracious and merciful, slow to anger, and of great kindness, and repenteth him of the evil.

Joel 2:12-13

The Shofar is an Instrument of Worship.

GOD'S WILL:
With trumpets and sound of cornet make a joyful noise before the Lord, the King.

Psalms 98:6

GOD'S WILL:
Praise him with the sound of the trumpet: praise him with the psaltery and harp.

Psalms 150:3

God is calling SOME to blow the Shofar and He is calling **ALL** to be human Shofars. To cry aloud, to lift up your voice, to let a dying world know about Jesus.

GOD'S WILL:
Cry aloud, spare not, lift up thy voice like a trumpet, and shew my people their transgression, and the house of Jacob their sins.

Isaiah 58:1

Is God calling you to blow the Shofar?

A teaching on "The Shofar"
is available on videotape.
See Item No. 3 on order form in back of book.

If you would like information on purchasing a shofar, check Item No.6 on order form in back of book.

ORDER FORM

Please send me:

SUGGESTED
LOVE OFFERING

1 ___ **"The Healing Testimony"** (from pg. 10) $5.00

2 ___ **"Equipping the Saints For The Work** $20.00
       of the Ministry"
       Series of four cassette tapes includes the
       following messages:
       Tape 1 Ministry of Reconciliation
       Tape 2 God Wants To Use Your Testimony
       Tape 3 Hearing God's Voice
       Tape 4 But One Thing Is Needful

3 ___ **"The Shofar" Video** (from pg. 33 & 112) $20.00
       The Shofar Video contains 3 teachings:
       # 1 The Trumpet Has Sounded — Repent!
       # 2 The Ordinance of the Shofar
       # 3 The Sound of The Shofar

4 ___ **"Jesus Gave Gifts"** (from pg. 41) $99.00
       Set of 5 Video's — 20 half-hour teachings on the Gifts of
       the Apostle, Prophet, Evangelist, Pastor, & Teacher.

5 ___ **"The Gift of the Evangelist - Parts 1 & 2"** $20.00
       (from pg. 53)

6 ___ Please send free information on purchasing a shofar.

To inquire about quantity pricing on
"DO YOU KNOW GOD'S WILL FOR YOUR LIFE?"
please write us at the address below.

Jim & Carla Barbarossa are scheduling
"Equipping the Saints" teaching seminars and "Do You
Know God's Will For Your Life?" meetings around the world.
For more information, write them at the address below.

Send order to:
Jim & Carla Barbarossa
Step by Step Ministries
215 Sauk Trail • Valparaiso, IN 46385

I am enclosing _____ plus 20% of the total price for postage
& handling. *(Overseas orders, please add 40% for postage)*

Name _____

Address _____

City/State/Zip _____

Phone ( ) _____